Caught in the Storm

Also Available from Lyceum Books, Inc.

Essential Skills of Social Work Practice:
Assessment, Intervention, and Evaluation
by Thomas O'Hare

Diversity, Oppression, and Change: Culturally Grounded Social Work
by Flavio Fransisco Marsiglia and Stephen Kulis

Complex Systems and Human Behavior
by Christopher G. Hudson

Community Health Care in Cuba
by Susan E. Mason, David L. Strug, and Joan Beder

Critical Multicultural Social Work
by Jose Sisneros, Catherine Stakeman, Mildred C. Joyner
and Cathryne L. Schmitz

Cross-Cultural Practice: Social Work With Diverse Populations
by Karen V. Harper and Jim Lantz

Women in Social Work Who Are Changing the World
by Alice Lieberman

Mindfulness and Social Work
by Steven F. Hick

CAUGHT IN THE STORM

NAVIGATING POLICY AND PRACTICE IN THE WELFARE REFORM ERA

Miguel Ferguson ■ *Heather Neuroth-Gatlin* ■ *Stacey Borasky*

LYCEUM
BOOKS, INC.
Chicago, Illinois

© 2010 by Lyceum Books, Inc.

Published by
LYCEUM BOOKS, INC.
5758 S. Blackstone Avenue
Chicago, Illinois 60637
773-643-1903 fax
773-643-1902 phone
lyceum@lyceumbooks.com
www.lyceumbooks.com

6   5   4   3   2   1   09   10   11   12   13

ISBN 978-1-933478-28-9

Printed in the United States of America.

Library of Congress Cataloging-in-Publication Data

Ferguson, Miguel.
Caught in the storm : navigating policy and practice in the welfare reform era / Miguel Ferguson, Heather Neuroth-Gatlin, Stacey Borasky.
    p.   cm.
ISBN 978-1-933478-28-9 (pbk. : alk. paper)
1. Social service—United States.   2. Social work administration—United States.   3. Public welfare—United States.   I. Neuroth-Gatlin, Heather.   II. Borasky, Stacey. III. Title.
HV91.F485   2010
362.5'820973—dc22
                                                                2009039777

Dedications

This book is dedicated to all of the brave women, men and children who have waded through the waters of welfare reform and Hurricane Katrina. Their courage, struggles, and fortitude in the face of hardship and disaster inspired this book.

To my parents, who taught me to value what is important; and my wife and children, who daily teach me what it means to love and be loved.

MF

To my loving and supportive husband, Travis: Thank you for the daily sacrifices you make to support my work and dreams. You inspire me to give more of myself every day, and I love you deeply.

HNG

To my parents, whose love and encouragement have been a lifelong gift. To my husband, whose love makes me a better person. And to my daughter, Hayley, who inspires me to make the world a better place for all children. I love you with all my heart.

SB

Contents

Acknowledgments

This book is the product of years of clinical practice, experience working in disaster relief in the aftermath of Hurricane Katrina, and a longitudinal program evaluation of welfare-to-work projects scattered throughout the Lone Star state and funded by the Texas Department of Human Services. Enormous thanks and gratitude are due to the "Welfare Innovation" project staff, who labored diligently to collect and share data on program participants and outcomes over a five-year period, and to a host of students and faculty colleagues who participated in the program evaluation in one important way or another: Dr. Diana DiNitto, Dr. Jim Schwab, Dr. Jinseok Kim, Dr. Melissa Radey, Dr. Dennis Poole, Dr. Seo-Koo Yoo, Dr. Kelly Alanis, Dr. Paul Muse Ritter, Mary Cook, Carla Gomez, Sabina Peerbhai, and Dina McLain.

We also wish to acknowledge staff from the University of Texas Center for Social Work Research (CSWR), Lutheran Social Services of the South (LSSS), FEMA, Lutheran Disaster Response, Katrina Aid Today, and coworkers from the University of Texas at Austin School of Social Work, and St. Edwards University. Finally, we extend our thanks and admiration to all nonprofit organizations in Texas, throughout the Gulf Coast, and across the country that work tirelessly to meet the needs of economically and emotionally stressed individuals and families. It is difficult to imagine the state of communities across this nation without the professionalism, dedication, and caring that these organizations bring to support those in need.

Abbreviations

RFP	Request for Proposals
ESL	English as a Second Language
TANF	Temporary Assistance for Needy Families
FBO	Faith-Based Organization
EITC	Earned Income Tax Credit
CHIP	Children's Health Insurance Program
FEMA	Federal Emergency Management Agency
WIC	Women, Infants, and Children program

Glossary of Policies,
Programs, and Terms

RFP: A Request for Proposals is an invitation for social service providers, often through a competitive process, to submit a proposal to provide services and/or resources to a defined population.

Bracero Program: A labor program initiated between the United States and Mexico during World War II, which culminated in millions of contract laborers from Mexico working in the U.S. agricultural sector.

Charitable Choice: Component of the Welfare Reform Act of 1996, which sought to reduce barriers to the receipt of federal funds on the part of faith-based organizations.

Office of Faith-Based and Community Initiatives: Established by an executive order from President George W. Bush on January 29, 2001.

Child Care Development Block Grant: Federal program that assists low-income families in obtaining childcare while working or in training.

Spanish Terms

Abuela: Grandmother.
Buena suerte: Good luck.
Buenas tardes: Good afternoon.
Bueno pues, porque yo no tengo nada: Good, because I have nothing.
Comida: Food.
¿De veras?: Really?
En una manera, es la misma cosa: In one way, it's the same thing.
¿Está en serio?: Are you serious?
Fíjate: Just imagine!
Hasta luego: See you later.
Hola: Hello.
Los pobres: The poor.
Mijo: My son (conjugation of "Mi hijo").
Momentito, por favor: Just a minute, please.
Qué calor!: It's so hot!
Sí, se puede: Yes, we can.
Tenemos una cita con Leticia a la una: We have an appointment with Leticia at 1:00 p.m.
Tengo sueño: I'm sleepy.
Tres leches: Sweet Mexican cake that translates literally as "three milks."

List of Characters

Martha	Executive Director of Helping Hands
Julia	Martha's Executive Assistant and single mother of two
Linda Devereaux	Caseworker, originally from New Orleans
David	Caseworker, social service as second career
Ruth	Social Services Coordinator, former NYC teacher born in the Dominican Republic
Evelyn	Tech support and part-time account manager
Melissa	Social work intern and eventual caseworker
Rev. Anderson	Outgoing minister whose church provides childcare for the Welfare-to-Work grant

Helping Hands Board Members

Carlos Hernandez	President of the Board, member of the Hispanic Chamber of Commerce, owner of local restaurant
Dr. Leta Shearer	Medical doctor who works at community clinic close to Helping Hands
Ronald Tripp	Attorney and past president of the board
Dr. Alvin Gault	Social Work professor
Carlene Francis	Former child welfare caseworker who now owns and operates a successful chain of flower shops

Foreword

Caught in the Storm tells the story of Helping Hands, a small nonprofit social service agency set in the fictional metropolis of River City. Readers will recognize Helping Hands as the type of agency where social workers are often employed to assist individuals and families to meet basic economic needs. In fact, many social workers have founded agencies like Helping Hands to meet pressing needs in their own communities. But *Caught in the Storm* stands in sharp contrast to didactic textbook accounts of agencies and their clients. It also differs from the accounts others have written of individuals trying to survive since Congress and President Bill Clinton ended welfare as we knew it. *Caught in the Storm* is most compelling in its use of narrative to tell the story of an agency, its staff, and its clients. The issues about social welfare policy and administration the authors have chosen to highlight emerge through action and dialogue among the book's characters. Readers will identify with Martha, the insightful and energetic executive director, as she and her staff reach out to other nonprofit and faith-based organizations to implement a welfare-to-work program, which will make a difference in the lives of the low-income clients they serve. *Caught in the Storm* also incorporates personal and ethical issues and political differences among staff and clients, revealing the day-to-day dramas with which social service agencies must deal even as they assume a larger role in the delivery of important social welfare services. Discussion questions and innovative assignments at the end of each chapter will also help instructors and students dig more deeply into the issues the book raises about the mechanisms currently being used to help people avoid or escape economic hardship.

I assisted in the evaluation of the welfare-to-work programs operated by community- and faith-based organizations that formed the basis of this book. I was with Miguel Ferguson when we ordered lunch through what we can only assume was bulletproof glass at a fast-food restaurant located near a project we evaluated in the fifth ward in Houston. I accompanied him when we interviewed coauthor Heather Neuroth-Gatlin, who ran one of the faith-based programs we evaluated and who later became a member of our evaluation team. I visited a residential substance abuse program that reminded me of the years

I spent working at a detoxification center and halfway house for people with alcohol and drug problems. I met with staff and clients of several other programs and love the way Miguel, Heather, and Stacey Borasky have woven what we heard and learned into the story of Helping Hands that you will read in this book. They have done a masterful job of writing a composite story of welfare-to-work programs, the individuals they aid, and the challenges they face.

I spent a good part of my childhood in South Florida and survived hurricanes in one of the oldest houses in our city. More than once we awoke to destruction from wind and water, but we were lucky to escape the devastation caused by hurricanes like Katrina and Rita. As the waters receded, Katrina and Rita uncovered stories of poverty and inequality that had not been exposed since the 1960s, when Michael Harrington's *The Other America* was published and Senators Robert F. Kennedy and Joseph Clark "discovered" hunger in our midst. As I write this foreword, the city of Galveston lies in ruin after Hurricane Ike, and once again it is tragically clear that we must be prepared not only to evacuate but to respond to basic human needs whenever natural disasters strike. These are the literal meanings of the title *Caught in the Storm*; but the title also has a figurative meaning. As dramatized in this artfully written book, *Caught in the Storm* can also be viewed as a metaphor for the devastation that problems like domestic violence and mortgage foreclosure wreak on the lives of Americans trying hard to provide for themselves and their families. The Helping Hands story is so compelling because the story isn't just fiction. The authors have written a true drama from the perspective of social service providers, and readers will both learn and be moved by what it has to share.

Diana DiNitto
Cullen Trust Centennial Professor in Alcohol Studies and Education
University Distinguished Teaching Professor
University of Texas at Austin School of Social Work

CHAPTER 1

An Opportunity Arises

JUNE 2004

Martha picked up the morning paper and headed to her car to face a congested thirty-minute commute across town to her westside office. Though it was early, the steering wheel was already hot to the touch. "Summer is definitely here," she thought, as she backed out of the driveway. As she left her middle-class neighborhood of spacious homes and nicely manicured lawns, the view quickly changed to the commercial billboards of the crosstown freeway. She exited onto a frontage road that slowly transformed into the low-income neighborhood surrounding her office. She had grown up in this area, and it pained her to see how it had deteriorated over the years.

As Martha drove by block after block of old wooden houses, fences in need of repair, and boarded-up, graffiti-covered buildings, she remembered that this had once been a solid working-class neighborhood with thriving family-owned businesses. But that was before the crosstown freeway had bisected the city and demarcated the west side as a place for the middleclass to avoid when possible. She drove by a low-income housing development where many of her clients lived. A few potted plants and cable television dishes did little to hide the poverty of the apartments. Wet laundry hung from balconies like white flags signaling surrender to the summer heat. Many of the houses had burglar bars bolted to the window frames, preventing any unwanted visitors from getting in—or any residents from getting out in an emergency. "Prisoners in their own homes," Martha sighed.

Martha approached her office, a one-story cinder block structure constructed in the 1960s. She was about to begin another day as Executive Director of Helping Hands, a small nonprofit social service agency that provided a variety of badly needed services to low-income families, such as emergency financial assistance, clothing, and food. In a city of almost one million people with a sizeable low-income population, Martha was only a small cog in the social service machinery, but she and her organization were dedicated to finding ways to help families in need. Martha was pragmatic, dedicated, and optimistic. The daughter of a decorated veteran who had relocated to the city after the Korean War, she was the first in her family to go to college. She had worked to pay her way through and eventually earned a Master of Social Work degree from the local state college.

There was never enough money to pay for the services that were so desperately needed, and this made Martha angry. There was no need in asking why. She had asked this question many times to no avail. Her small staff had been putting in overtime as the summer began, with nearly twice as many clients requesting utility assistance compared with the rest of the year. The case managers had been staying after hours to process extra paperwork, and the volunteer coordinator, a new social work intern, had held numerous training sessions in the evenings in the past month to bring more volunteers in to help with the increased workload. But it still wasn't enough.

Martha reflected on her five years as Executive Director. She came to the job in the midst of an economic boom and right after the state had enacted a new set of welfare reform policies. Her goals then were to solidify funding of Helping Hands' core programs and explore new ways to help the agency expand its mission to assist families in their transition from public assistance and out of poverty. But jobs, especially full-time jobs with benefits, were much harder to find now, making it increasingly challenging for clients to achieve and maintain self-sufficiency. The agency's financial situation began to deteriorate when the downturn in the economy and in the stock market severely reduced funding from the individuals and foundations upon which the agency depended. This was followed by across-the-board cuts, mandated by the legislature, in state funding of social services—cuts that were aligned with the new governor's campaign pledge not to raise taxes to meet the state's looming shortfall. The intractable situation dominated the conversation at a United Way meeting Martha had recently attended: when the need for services goes up, the resources available to social service agencies invariably go down.

Martha focused on her surroundings as she pulled into the agency parking lot. Most of the cars were older models, marked by rust and tires with thinning treads. It was 7:45 a.m. and already several clients were waiting for the doors to open at 8. "The first of the month," thought Martha. The beginning and end of the month always found the agency inundated with clients: rent and utilities were due.

Martha drove to the rear of the building and parked. As usual, she was the first staff member to arrive. She opened the door and headed down the long corridor to her office, turning the lights on as she went. She made a mental note that the walls looked dingy and in need of a new coat of paint. She reached the end of the hallway, turned on the air conditioner, and entered her office.

Looking over messages from the previous day, Martha looked out her window and saw Julia's car enter the parking lot. Julia was Martha's administrative assistant and the glue that held the office together. Martha noted that Julia's car wasn't in much better shape than the others in the lot. A single mother of two teenage boys, Julia had recently moved from Atlanta to be closer to family after her divorce. Although she had worked at Helping Hands for less than a year, her sharp wit and dedication made her indispensable.

Martha made notations in her planner about the day's tasks: nine a.m. staff meeting, a brown-bag lunch meeting with the board of directors at noon, and then an afternoon of what she hoped would be productive grant writing. Martha looked over a funding opportunity she had downloaded from a state agency Web site over the weekend: the Workforce Development Board had issued a Request for Proposals (RFP) to local community- and faith-based organizations to apply for funding to implement innovative welfare-to-work programs. She started thinking about how she could best broach this new funding opportunity to the board of directors later in the day. Could it be the answer to her prayers?

"Need anything for the staff meeting, Martha?" Julia popped her head around the door and eyed the stacks of paper on Martha's desk and filing cabinets.

"Yes, could you make copies of these for everyone, please?" Martha handed her the agenda and a copy of the RFP, then gathered her papers and headed for the conference room. On the way, Martha saw that two of the case managers, Linda and David, were getting the food pantry ready and sorting clothes for the small "closet" that Helping Hands maintained. Linda Devereaux was twenty-four years old, single, and fresh out of Tulane University, where she had just earned a master's degree in social work. Linda was a bundle of energy and a triathlete whose enthusiasm often outweighed her experience. David was thirty-two years old and pursuing social service work as a second career. He had worked in pharmaceutical sales after getting a degree in biology and lived with his long-time partner. At first he had viewed the temporary position at Helping Hands as a transitional form of employment, but enjoyed the work so much that he had recently accepted a full-time position. In the pharmaceutical industry, he had enjoyed a high salary, a company car, and an expense account. Now he took pleasure in helping those who sought his services, rather than aggressively pursuing customers over a broad sales region. He had recently taken the step of requesting program information from several graduate schools of social work.

Ruth, the social services coordinator, entered through the back door, her arms full of paperwork. She said hello and rushed past everyone to drop some papers at her desk, then quickly returned to pour herself a cup of coffee. Ruth was the no-nonsense matriarch of the group and loved to gush about the latest antics of her grandchildren. A first-generation U.S. citizen, her family had emigrated from the Dominican Republic in 1965 due to the political turbulence and shortly after U.S. marines sent by President Johnson had landed on the island. She had taught Spanish and drama for twenty years in New York City public schools. Her claim to fame was that she had once been a student of Frank McCourt, long before he had achieved celebrity and success as the author of *Angela's Ashes*. When her husband took a job in River City, she chose to work at a nonprofit in order to continue serving low-income populations. She was writing a book about her teaching experiences and was actively involved in community education and literacy issues.

The tech support and default accounts manager, Evelyn, (whom everyone referred to as Evy) and Melissa, the social work intern, arrived a few minutes later. Julia passed out copies of the agenda and RFP.

Evelyn had a bachelor's degree in accounting from a small public university and specialized in providing contract assistance to small nonprofits. Once an auditor in a well-known accounting firm, Evelyn now balanced work and motherhood by operating a consulting firm part-time out of her home. She did contract work with Helping Hands and other social service agencies while taking care of twins—a maternal characteristic that she and Martha had in common. Melissa, a social work intern from Martha's alma mater, looked up to Martha and hoped one day to start her own nonprofit agency working with chronically ill children. She was bright and dedicated. Martha recognized her potential and, recalling her own formative internship experience at a residential care facility, resolved to make Melissa's internship as meaningful as possible.

Melissa sat across from Ruth and smiled. Although she had just started her summer internship as the volunteer coordinator, she had quickly become an integral part of the agency team. Martha appreciated her exuberance and wondered if she had been as energetic when she had been an intern. The energy and new ideas that students brought to the job made the extra responsibility of supervising student interns worthwhile.

Martha covered minor details with her staff before launching into the funding issue. "As you know, our financial situation is critical. Some of our major funding sources have been cut, and I'm not sure how much longer we'll be able to maintain the services we now provide. I've been looking for new funding sources and just came across an RFP that is due at the end of the month."

"Where is it from?" asked Ruth.

Martha could see that the staff was interested. "The RFP is from the Workforce Development Board. They want nonprofits and faith-based organizations to establish innovative social service programs that either assist people in exiting the welfare system or help prevent them from getting on welfare in the first place."

David chimed in, "That's great, but how do they define 'innovative'?"

Martha smiled. "Good question. It appears they're interested in new services, new partnerships, and new ways of delivering services."

Linda spoke up, "Could we use this to provide more financial assistance? Our clients aren't going to be able to leave welfare or find employment if they're worried about being evicted or getting their utilities cut off."

"What about transportation?" asked David.

"Educational services could also be packaged in innovative ways," said Ruth, getting excited about the idea of creating an English as a Second Language program that would link existing agencies.

Martha added, "Those are some really good ideas. Anything else come to mind?"

"What about a client survey?" Melissa piped in. "Would we have enough time to come up with one? It could really help."

"That's a definite possibility," Martha replied. "But we would have to put it together quickly."

"We already have a basic interview questionnaire that we administer to all new clients," said Linda. "Could we just use that?"

"I'd like to expand on it a bit, maybe ask a few more questions about hardships they're experiencing and what they would need to make a transition from welfare to work," Martha added.

"Or keep them from going on welfare," Julia added, noting the wording in the RFP, which specified that all households under 150 percent of the poverty level with children under the age of eighteen, not just those receiving public assistance, would be eligible.

"Good point," Martha affirmed. "Though the RFP seems geared toward moving folks off TANF, the income eligibility ceiling will cover a lot of the working poor as well."

"I don't know if you want to do any telephone interviews," said Evelyn, "but I could download some interview software from the Web if you like. Once you have the questions, we could paste them in and be ready to go."

"Thanks Evy," Martha replied. Though Evelyn was primarily responsible for the budget and accounts, she sometimes provided technical support as well.

The staff was clearly ready to create new and innovative ways to serve Helping Hands' clients. Martha considered herself quite fortunate to have such a talented and team-oriented crew. In her career, she had worked at agencies that were riven with personality conflicts and turf issues, places where workers were likely to say they were too busy to put something together in a pinch or demand credit or control of the process. Though Martha was confident in her ability to recognize and hire good employees, she knew a certain amount of luck was involved in building a staff that worked so well together.

She ended the meeting with some positive comments. "I think we're off to a good start. Keep thinking about how the kinds of services we propose can meet emergency needs and create real opportunities for our clients. I'm going to pitch this funding opportunity to the board this afternoon. I hope they're as enthusiastic as you!"

After the meeting, Martha went back to her office and began to devise a plan for the grant. She knew the board was wary of her applying for every funding opportunity that crossed her desk, so she outlined answers to questions they would most likely ask. She wanted to be ready for them.

Just before noon, Martha could hear the board members greet her staff as they entered the lobby. She was fortunate; every person on the board was committed to the success of the agency's mission. Each was an established professional in the community and dedicated a good deal of expertise and time to the agency. Although they were supportive, they could also be very demanding, and some of them always seemed to lean on the side of caution at the expense of innovation. She hoped she could convince them of the benefits of this opportunity.

"Good afternoon, Martha!" said criminal defense attorney Ronald Tripp, a past president of the board. He was usually all business, but seemed to be in a particularly good mood. "Good," thought Martha, "maybe that'll be a plus on my side." Ronald was a good member to have on her team. He was meticulous and wary of making large decisions without research and study. He tended to think of problems before solutions, but he was a good watchdog for the board.

As the board members began to seat themselves in the conference room and open their box lunches, Martha heard Carlos Hernandez greet Ruth in Spanish. Carlos was president of the board and a member of the Hispanic Business Association. As a child, Carlos had come to the United States with his parents during the *Bracero* program, which operated during World War II. *Bracero* was the term given to tens of thousands of guest workers from Mexico who worked in the agricultural sector during the war and for years afterwards. Carlos was proud of his family history and frequently reminded those around him that Mexican laborers had contributed vitally to the war effort and continued to play an important role in the U.S. economy. Carlos often hosted agency functions at his well-known family restaurant and provided a tremendous link to the Hispanic community.

Carlos sat next to Dr. Leta Shearer, a primary-care physician and mother of two, who somehow found time to sit on the board. An adjunct faculty member at the medical school, Dr. Shearer worked at a community clinic a few blocks from Helping Hands. She was an outspoken advocate for a national health care system and often provided care for clients from Helping Hands.

Dr. Alvin Gault, a social work professor from the local university, was looking over the agenda. With his beard and burly build, Dr. Gault looked more like a lumberjack than a college professor. He had evaluated many social service programs and had strong opinions about what worked and what didn't. He could be overly intellectual at times but knew the social service arena and always made good points. His research focused on poverty and welfare policy. He had recommended Melissa, one of his students, for the internship with Martha at Helping Hands. Martha made a mental note to thank him because Melissa was already a great asset.

Next to him, Carlene Francis, a local businesswoman, chatted with Dr. Shearer about their children. Carlene had once been a colleague of Martha's at Children's Services, but was now a successful entrepreneur, having nurtured a string of flower shops into a small franchise. Carlene had three children: two girls in high school and a son who was doing a tour of duty in Iraq. She had recently attended the funeral service of a friend of her son who had enlisted with him after high school. He had been killed in April when his convoy struck a roadside bomb outside of Fallujah; Carlene lived in constant fear that she would someday suffer the loss of her soldier son. While he was away, his young wife and one-year-old baby lived with her. Carlene liked to say that her house was filled with the most beautiful things in life: flowers and children.

Carlos began the meeting. For the first ten minutes they reviewed the account of the last meeting, talked about doing some minor repairs and upkeep on the building, and then began to discuss funding.

Martha wasted no time. "I've come across an opportunity that could significantly increase the agency's funding base and help provide needed services to clients." She knew she had their full attention and continued, describing in some detail the innovative welfare-to-work RFP she had recently discovered. She explained the basic parameters of the grant, which generally aligned with the mission of Helping Hands, and the sizeable amount of money available.

Ronald immediately spoke up. "I know we could use the money, Martha, and I'm all for providing innovative services to clients . . .

"Well," thought Martha, "there goes Ronald's good mood."

"It takes a lot of effort to start a new program," he continued. "Is there any guarantee that the funding won't be pulled in one or two years?"

"You're being too cautious, Ronald," said Dr. Shearer, jumping into the conversation. She had seen too many desperate families in the clinic recently not to be alert to the possibilities offered by this proposal. "First, I think this grant could actually help us achieve our mission in a way that we're really not doing now. We're just stretched too thin. Second, Martha has done an outstanding job leading this agency. If she thinks she can make this work, then I think we should let her move ahead with it."

"I have no doubt that Martha is aware of the community's needs, and I know that she would make a good assessment prior to plunging ahead," said Professor Gault, leafing through the RFP. "But with all due respect, I think this is the perfect time to be forthright with our concerns. I'm apprehensive about the eligibility restrictions in this contract. Although the extra financial assistance would certainly be of great benefit to certain clients, what will you say to other clients who can't receive these special services? Don't you think this would give the impression that we're favoring certain people?"

Before Martha could answer, Professor Gault brought up one more point. "Besides the service delivery issue, the RFP mentions that an evaluation is going to be done on every program that receives funds. I've conducted many program evaluations, and I probably don't have to tell you that government contracts often come with some rigorous reporting requirements. If you apply for this funding, that's definitely something to keep in mind."

Martha nodded her head as she listened to all the concerns. She wanted them to know that she valued their time and input. "As usual, you've all raised some very good issues. And if we decide to apply for funding, I want you to know that my staff and I will do everything we can to incorporate your concerns into our service delivery proposal. But at the same time, I feel that the extra funding could help us put together a program that would really make a difference in our clients' lives. I think it would also allow us to be proactive rather than just respond to emergency needs as they come up."

Various board members nodded in agreement, but Carlos had a concerned look on his face.

"Marta, Professor Gault brought up a good point. This contract requires proof of U.S. citizenship. We've worked hard to develop the trust of the Latino community. Once we start demanding proof of citizenship, we could lose the ground we've gained."

"That's one of the first things that came to mind when I read the announcement, Carlos," said Martha. "There are a number of ways for us to approach this. We could ask the Workforce Development Board to provide referrals to our project. If the clients are screened for eligibility before they are referred to us, we can avoid that problem and maintain our open-door policy. Or we could screen through other methods that would help us to maintain our community trust." Carlos and the other board members nodded in approval. Martha's preparation for the board's concerns seemed to be paying off.

Carlene offered some positive encouragement. "I think all these problems have solutions. I know the problems some of my employees are having with childcare and transportation. I imagine it's even more so for women who are trying to leave the welfare system. The RFP says that the maximum allowable amount per year is two hundred and fifty thousand dollars. That's a good chunk of money! I'm with Leta—I don't think we should hesitate on this one."

"Since the proposal is due in less than a month, there's not much time to waste," Martha replied. "Would you be able to look over a rough draft as soon as we can put it together?" she asked, looking at each board member. They all nodded in agreement.

"Well," said Ronald, swallowing his last bite of sandwich, "before we give you the green light, are you thinking of expanding the number of staff or partnering with other agencies?"

"The RFP emphasized community partnerships, and I think it would be easier to cooperate with other agencies than try and reinvent the wheel." Martha began to explain.

"Especially on such short notice," interjected Professor Gault. Martha was relieved that Ronald seemed satisfied with the explanations.

Looking at her watch, Dr. Shearer asked "Where to from here, Martha?"

"My staff is ready to work on a needs-assessment survey targeted at the low-income populations we want to serve. The responses we get should shed some light on what services are needed the most."

"I think that will strengthen the application, too," said Professor Gault, cutting in again.

The members nodded, and Martha continued. "In the meantime, I'm going to make some calls and see if other agencies would like to work with us on this project. I already have a few in mind." Martha waited for more questions, but the board members, finally, seemed to be satisfied.

Carlene laughed, "Ron, when are you going to realize that Martha is always one step ahead of you?"

"I think that goes for all of us," said Dr. Shearer, smiling.

"Are there any more concerns?" asked Carlos, looking around the room to make sure that everyone had one last chance to speak.

"Other than this box lunch, I don't have any," joked Carlene. "I say we have our next board meeting at your place, Carlos!"

"Agreed," said Carlos, looking around the room, "I guess you have unanimous approval. *¡Buena suerte*, Marta!"

Questions for Discussion

1. On her drive to work, Martha notes that the neighborhood in which she grew up had significantly deteriorated. What are some of the negative physical characteristics that have commonly come to be associated with low-income neighborhoods? What are some of the negative behavioral characteristics that have commonly come to be associated with residents of low-income neighborhoods? Do you believe these characteristics are accurate or false? Why?

2. What kind of taxes do state and local governments rely on to fund social programs? How are these taxes susceptible to downturns in the local economy?

3. Should state and local taxes be progressive; that is, based on an individual or household's ability to pay, or should the same (flat) rate be applied to everyone, regardless of income?

4. In many states, nonprofit agencies like Helping Hands form a crucial part of the social service safety net and are significant actors in the local economy. What advantages, for example, in customer service or administrative efficiency, would a local organization like Helping Hands have over a large government bureaucracy? In what ways might small agencies like Helping Hands be at a disadvantage?

5. A significant portion of nonprofit social service agency budgets comes in the form of grants and contracts (as opposed to private charitable donations). What are the advantages and disadvantages of such types of funding? To clients? To agencies? To funding sources and communities?

6. The grant from the Workforce Board requires funded agencies to cooperate with an external program evaluation. What are the advantages of a formal program evaluation? What are the potential disadvantages?

7. How can social workers and public administrators play a role in shaping political decisions made by legislators? Do you think training in political decision-making processes should be a mandatory part of social work and public administration education? Why or why not?

Innovative Assignments

1. Collect three to five mission statements from local nonprofit organizations in your community, which provide services to low-income populations. Describe the history, size, and scope of the organizations, the services each provides, sources of funding, and the populations each serves. Describe any unique organizational or service features. What sort of strengths or weaknesses seem apparent from the information provided? Next, using the mission statements you have collected as guides, write a brief mission statement for Helping Hands.

2. As a new intern for a local nonprofit organization, you have been asked by the executive director to prepare a brief PowerPoint summary of the major demographic characteristics of the community in which the agency is located. The executive director suggests that you use the Census Bureau's American Community Survey (http://www.census.gov/) and organize the data at the county level. Though you may want to include additional information, your summary should include details about household composition, age, marital status, children, fertility, school enrollment and educational attainment, citizenship and ethnic status, employment and income, cost of housing, homeownership status, and poverty levels.

Suggested Readings

Alexander, J. (2003). The impact of devolution on nonprofits. *Nonprofit Management and Leadership, 10*(1), 57–70.

Alvarez, L., & Wilson, M. (2009, May 29). Up and out of New York's projects. *The New York Times.* Available at http://www.endowmentnyc.org/download/nyt_up_and_out_article.pdf

Brooks, A. C. (2004). The effects of public policy on private charity. *Administration & Society, 36,* 166–185.

Chait, R. P., Ryan, W. P., & Taylor, B. E. (2005). *Governance as leadership: Reframing the work of nonprofit boards.* Hoboken, NJ: Wiley.

DeParle, J. (2004). *American dream: Three women, ten kids, and a nation's drive to end welfare.* New York: Viking.

Kissane, R. J., & Gingerich, J. (2004). Do you see what I see? Nonprofit and resident perceptions of their neighborhoods. *Nonprofit and Voluntary Sector Quarterly, 33*(2), 311–333.

Light, P. (2004). *Sustaining nonprofit performance: The case for capacity building and the evidence to support it.* Washington, DC: Brookings Institution Press.

Linden, R. M. (2002). *Working across boundaries: Making collaboration work in government and nonprofit organizations.* San Francisco: Jossey-Bass.

Peck, L. (2008). Do antipoverty nonprofits locate where people need them? Evidence from a spatial analysis of Phoenix. *Nonprofit and Voluntary Sector Quarterly, 37,* 138–151.

Penniman, N. (2001, November 5). Wealth of spirit: Will nonprofits be a casualty of war? *The American Prospect, 12*(19). Available at http://www.prospect.org/cs/articles?article = wealth_of_spirit

Rushton, M., & Brooks, A. C. (2006). Government funding of nonprofit organizations. In D. R. Young (Ed.), *Financing nonprofits: Putting theory into practice* (pp. 69–92). Lanham, MD: Altamira Press.

Schin, J., & McClomb, G. E. (1998). Top executive leadership and organizational innovation: An investigation of nonprofit human service organizations. *Social Work Administration, 22*(3), 1–21.

Schneider, J. (2006). *Social capital and welfare reform: Organizations, congregations, and communities.* New York: Columbia University Press.

Smith, S., & Lipsky, M. (1993). *Nonprofits for hire: The welfare state in the age of contracting.* Cambridge, MA: Harvard University Press.

CHAPTER 2

A Question of Needs

JUNE 15, 2004

Martha leaned back in her chair, stretched, and rotated her neck several times to get the kinks out. She had been sitting at her desk for hours reading comments clients had made while completing the needs-assessment surveys. After receiving the go-ahead from the board of directors to apply for the welfare-to-work grant, Martha and her staff had worked diligently to design a short survey that identified barriers to employment and material hardships that Helping Hands' clients faced. Over the past week, Melissa had conducted phone surveys with clients who had received agency services in the past month, and David completed surveys during intake interviews with clients requesting agency services for the first time. Together they had completed nearly one hundred surveys, which Melissa had conveniently packaged in an Excel file, complete with summary statistics. Martha never ceased to be amazed at how quickly technology had changed since she had begun working in the social services. As she sat on the edge of her chair and stretched her legs under the desk, she remembered using typewriters and making copies with carbon paper while working at various agencies in college. "Makes me feel like a dinosaur" she thought to herself.

She got up and headed to the break room for a final cup of coffee. Though it was well after five o'clock, she was surprised to find David and Melissa sitting at the table.

"Are you two still here?" Martha was glad to see that there was still some coffee in the pot. She grabbed a mug and poured herself the last cup.

"Actually, we were just discussing the client survey," said Melissa.

"Thanks again for arranging the data in that Excel file for me, Melissa. It's been a big help. It must have taken a while for you to do all that."

"Actually, it wasn't that hard," Melissa explained, "especially after Evy showed me a few tricks. Now I'd like to put the data in SPSS and run some correlations that I learned in Dr. Gault's class last semester."

"I'll make sure to tell Dr. Gault the next time I see him," Martha said with a smile.

"Well, I never took a research methods class," said David, "but it's pretty clear that our clients have a lot of needs going unmet. I mean, I work with them everyday, and I was still surprised by some of their responses."

"What surprised you the most?" Martha asked as she took a seat at the table.

"I was a little surprised at how big a problem transportation is," David stated as he shuffled through some pages of the summary statistics. "Even though the city bus system is pretty good, people are having a hard time affording bus fare—or it takes them hours to go from their house to childcare and then to work. And with gas prices going over two dollars a gallon, I mean, a tank of gas costs a lot more than it did last summer. Maybe we could offer monthly bus fare or gas vouchers or even car repairs to help clients get to their jobs or look for work."

"I think the survey has given all of us some surprises," Martha said in reply. "I'm glad we asked about future employment plans as part of the survey. I was a bit surprised at the number of people who said they needed help paying for things like testing and license application fees, and even textbooks and special uniforms." Despite their daily experience working with the agency's clients, the process of conducting the surveys and asking pointed questions about barriers to employment had clearly been a valuable use of time.

"What about you, Melissa? Were you surprised by anything in particular from the surveys?" Martha asked.

"Well, I didn't realize just how complicated the whole childcare thing would be," Melissa answered.

"In what way?" queried Martha.

"I mean, I knew there was a long waiting list for government subsidized programs, but even clients *with* childcare have issues. It's expensive, and it's not offered at times when a lot of them have to work, like weekends or evenings. And though it wasn't part of the survey, a number of them told me that they would be able to work more, or take better paying jobs, if they had access to night or weekend care."

"So if you need the money, or for whatever reason that's your only option, what do families do?" asked David.

"They do what lots of families do," said Martha. "After school the kids stay home alone, or the older kids take care of the younger ones; and if you work a night or weekend shift, you hope a family member or a neighbor can help you out. Did you hear about the mother whose two children recently drowned while she was working a double shift?"

"We talked about that in my child welfare class," said Melissa, sadly shaking her head.

"What happened?" asked David.

"Well," said Melissa, "she was a single mom with four kids. I think the oldest was twelve. Anyway, she was working and the twelve-year-old was supposed to be watching the kids. Somehow, one of them, I think the little girl, who was about two, got out and fell into the pool at the apartment complex, which was full of brackish water. When the twelve-year-old figured out what had happened, she jumped in to save her but ended up drowning too. CPS took custody of her other children," she added in a rueful tone.

"And the mother was arrested," added Martha.

"Oh my God, that's awful," said David, shaking his head.

"And that's why we had to be careful about what questions to include on the survey," Martha said as she stared into her cup, which was now almost empty. "Asking for help is hard enough. And I certainly didn't want to ask first-time clients the kinds of questions where honest answers could get them in trouble. It's enough to establish that they have childcare needs going unmet."

"I see your point," said David.

The weight of the conversation took its toll on the group. After a moment of silence had passed, David got up from the table and grabbed another soda from the refrigerator.

Melissa returned to the conversation. "If I had kids, I don't know what I would do if I had to leave them someplace that I didn't feel good about. What did you do when Brandon and Jessie were little?" she asked Martha.

"I was lucky," Martha replied. "When the twins were born, my husband and I decided that, although I had a job as a caseworker, most of my salary would have gone toward daycare. So it just made sense to stay home with them until they started preschool."

"Keeping up with twins all day long? Wears me out just thinking about it," David said as he sat back down at the table.

"Where do you think the gray hair comes from?" laughed Martha. "But I feel lucky to have been able to stay with them, and my parents helped out quite a lot."

"In the child welfare class I took last semester, my professor mentioned that a year of full-time care for an infant is often more expensive than a year of college tuition," said Melissa.

"Are you kidding?" replied David, incredulously.

"No, that's true," Martha answered. "Licensed childcare for infants runs about two hundred dollars a week. Sometimes more."

"Two hundred bucks a week? Wait a minute, two-hundred bucks a week, fifty weeks a year, that's ten grand a year! A full-time worker making the minimum of five-fifteen an hour would only make about two hundred dollars a week, and that's *before* taxes," David continued while shaking his head.[1] "Why would anyone with children work for that amount? It doesn't make sense!"

"Well, they work because they don't have any other way to pay for food and shelter," Martha replied.

---

[1] The federal minimum wage, originally established in 1938, was increased in July 2007 to $5.85, in July 2008 to $6.55, and in July 2009 to $7.25.

"That sounds like a setup to me," decried David, putting his soda down noisily on the table. "If you work at a low-wage job, you can't afford childcare, and if you don't work, you can't afford anything! No wonder our clients are having such a tough time!"

"Well, that's certainly a big part of it," Martha replied. "Unlike other benefits, the minimum wage is not automatically adjusted for inflation, so it doesn't have the purchasing power it once had," she said. "You know, both of my parents worked minimum wage jobs at one point or another when I was growing up, but I don't remember things being so bad. At any rate, it just wouldn't be possible in this day and age."

"When was the last time it was raised?" asked David.

"I should know this," Melissa said, "but I'm drawing a blank."

"Don't worry, Melissa," Martha said with a smile. "I won't tell Dr. Gault." Turning to David, Martha paused for a moment. "It was raised twice during the Clinton administration, but I'm not sure what exact years. I read an article recently that made the case that Clinton's ability to raise the minimum wage after the 1994 conservative takeover was testament to his political skills."

"Speaking of conservatives," David continued, "I remember my dad railing against all the money people on welfare were getting. In fact, I'm pretty sure that's why he voted for Reagan. I remember him saying that Reagan was going to cut the free lunch that made so many people lazy."

Martha listened intently. David was a relatively new employee and she was glad he felt comfortable discussing the often-contentious subjects that were crucial to the well-being of the clients that Helping Hands served. "Well, most of the folks we help do receive some form of government assistance, but it's rarely enough to really make ends meet," she answered. "That's why they come to Helping Hands. Just look at our survey responses. Many of them receive food stamps, but they still run short on food at the end of the month, which is why our pantry is always so busy at that time. And did you know that the minimum food stamp allotment is just ten dollars a month?[2] That's what it was back when I was a social work intern like Melissa!"

"Well," David interjected, "my dad would say that they ran short because they were buying steaks on the taxpayer's dime."

"Wait a minute, can I go back to the ten-dollar thing?" asked Melissa, perking up. "In my social-policy class, we went over an application for food stamps that was eight pages long. Then we had a guest speaker talk to us about all the information and identification that applicants have to bring to an eligibility interview: social security cards, pay stubs, bank statements, rent or mortgage papers, car titles, et cetera. So the caseworker has to look at all this paperwork, and the applicant has to take time off work to show up for an

---

[2] Monthly minimum and maximum benefit levels were increased in April 2009 as part of President Barack Obama's economic stimulus efforts.

interview for what might only amount to *ten* dollars of food stamps?" Melissa asked with disbelief.

"That can't be what most people get, because no sane person would go through all that for ten bucks," exclaimed David.

Martha acknowledged David's skepticism. "You're right, David. I was referring to the minimum; the *average* benefit level for food stamps is about eighty-five dollars per person per month. And it does help, no doubt about it. The switch from having to use a booklet of stamps to a state-issued debit card has helped too. But the process is cumbersome and it takes so long to actually get food stamps that about half the people who are eligible don't even bother to apply."

"Well, if half of those who are eligible don't receive benefits, does that mean that they didn't really need the benefits that much in the first place? And wouldn't that save the government a lot of money?" queried David.

Martha enjoyed David's questioning nature and nodded her head in reply. "In my opinion, the means test should be composed of the questions on the application, not the process itself. And with regard to your second question, since the federal government pays for all the benefits and half the administrative costs, it really means that the state and local communities *lose* a lot of money. Honestly, I'm surprised that grocery stores don't do more outreach to help people apply for food stamps. They potentially lose millions of dollars each month. Just doesn't make sense to me."

"Wow," said David, "I didn't know it worked that way." He took a gulp of his soda. "But you mentioned a means test. What's that?"

"It's the test the government or an agency applies to determine if an individual or household's means, that is, their income or assets, are limited enough to merit assistance," Martha explained.

"Oh, I get it," said David, "literally, a test of their means."

Melissa found the entire conversation eye-opening. She had known that the Food Stamps program wasn't serving everyone that it could, but hadn't fully understood the collective economic impact that individual decisions could have on the broader community. In her social work classes, she had often heard the phrase "the personal is political" repeated, but realized now that it was not just a cliché.

"All this talk about food has made me hungry," David said.

"Well, my husband is working late tonight and the twins are with my parents, so why don't we continue the conversation over dinner?" Martha offered. "It's the least I can do to thank you for getting the surveys done so quickly."

"Really, you don't have to," said Melissa. "I learned a lot from doing these surveys."

"I'm glad you learned a lot, Melissa" Martha interjected, "but the work you have done will give us a leg up on this application. I think the Workforce

Board will be impressed that we conducted a needs assessment and based our welfare-to-work plan on our findings."

"Hey, I'm willing to accept food as payment for a job well done!" David joked. They all laughed.

Twenty minutes later they were seated in a corner booth at Casa Yucateca, the restaurant owned by Helping Hands board member Carlos Hernandez. The restaurant specialized in cuisine from the Yucatán, and Martha always enjoyed their seafood and delicious lime soup, selections that were not available at other Mexican restaurants in River City.

Carlos spotted Martha from the kitchen and made his way across the dining room to say hello. Martha introduced him to David and Melissa and gave Carlos a quick update on the status of the grant application. He was impressed with the progress they had made, and shared his pleasure at seeing Helping Hands make an effort to expand its services in such a meaningful way. Carlos asked the waitress to bring three bowls of lime soup, which he knew was Martha's favorite, and shared some of his family history with them as they waited.

"My grandfather was of Mayan descent, and grew up in a small fishing village on Isla Mujeres, near Cancún, long before it became a world renowned resort," said Carlos.

"I went to Cancún on spring break during college," David said, "but we ended up spending all our time in Tulum. It was just beautiful," he added, somewhat wistfully.

"Ah, you are a smart man, Señor David," responded Carlos. "The ruins at Tulum, Chichén Itzá, and Uxmal are some of the most breathtaking in the world. I did not see them myself until I was a grown man."

"Why is that?" asked Melissa.

Carlos paused, as if remembering the circumstances as they had originally been shared with him. "A hurricane destroyed my grandfather's boat, and he and my father decided to try their luck in *El Norte* during the war years," he recounted. Surveying the beautifully decorated interior of his restaurant, he added, "I guess all their hard work paid off."

"Yes, it did," said Martha. "You have the best restaurant in River City."

"You are too kind, Señora Marta!" Carlos gushed. Martha always enjoyed the way Carlos pronounced her name. Between the regional cuisine and Carlos' charm and hospitality, it was no wonder that Casa Yucateca was always busy, Martha thought.

The waitress arrived with steaming bowls of lime soup. Carlos reiterated his pleasure in seeing Martha and meeting David and Melissa, and admonished them to save room for his brother's famous *tres leches* cake.

During dinner, the conversation took a detour as Melissa shared a story about a client she had helped earlier in the day. She had mentioned it to Ruth, who encouraged her to talk about it with Martha.

"Uh, Martha, I'd like to get some input from you on something that happened today," she began.

"Of course," responded Martha. From the meticulous way Melissa folded her napkin before speaking, Martha could see it was not going to be the run-of-the-mill type of question that interns often asked after joining Helping Hands.

"This morning a woman came into the office needing some financial assistance. She said she just moved to town a few weeks ago and was having trouble finding a job. I ended up giving her a utility voucher and a week's worth of food from the pantry. She had a young son, and her husband had left her and wasn't paying any child support. She didn't even know where he was to try to get it from him. She cried the whole time she was in my office, and I just felt awful for her." Melissa paused as she considered what to say next. "But that's not what I want to talk about," she added.

"Oh, okay," replied Martha, trying to sound supportive.

Melissa again smoothed the napkin on her lap and glanced at David, who nudged her on with a look.

"Well, I haven't shared this before, but this client and our conversation tonight make me feel I should tell you," Melissa began.

"Is this something we should keep confidential?" Martha asked gently.

Melissa continued. "It's really not a problem if others know, but I didn't realize how much working at Helping Hands would bring up my own issues. My mom was on welfare when I was young, from the time I was in preschool until I finished third grade. I have vague memories of that time, but Mom and I have talked about it a lot since I started in the social work program. To make a long story short, when my parents divorced, Mom had to start over, so we moved to a larger town where she thought she might have more chances at a good job. She had some experience doing office work, but she never went to college. She worked two jobs and had neighbors take care of me and my little sister until she could make enough money to drop one of the jobs. We got food stamps until I was about eight years old. Mom was able to earn a promotion and made enough money so she could drop one job. We kept getting food stamps for a while after that."

Melissa took a deep breath and went on. "Anyway, the client who came in today reminded me of my mom. There was a part of me that wanted to tell her that it really is possible to have a better life, since my mom was able to do it." Melissa paused and waited for some reaction from the others.

Martha looked intently at Melissa. "Are you wondering whether or not it was okay to share that story with your client?" she asked.

"Well, we've talked about self-disclosure in class, but I don't feel like I really know the whole 'boundary' issue that well," she responded. "It just seems hard not to react emotionally, but I think I did all right with that today. I mean, I didn't tell her my story or anything, but would it have been so bad if I did?"

Martha replied to Melissa's question. "There will always be times when a client's situation will be similar to your own or bring out certain emotions from your own experiences. But professionals should only share their feelings or personal background when doing so is for the clear benefit of the client. Otherwise, as a general rule of thumb, it's just not appropriate."

Melissa nodded her understanding. "But how do you make that distinction? I really do think it would have helped her to know that while moving to a new town brings real challenges, it is possible, with help from agencies like ours and determination, to find work that helps you take care of your family and feel better about yourself."

Martha could see that the issue of self-disclosure needed to be clarified. "Let me give you two examples of self-disclosure, one good, and one bad," she continued, gesturing with her right hand and then with her left hand to make the point. "Let's assume a client has just shared with a worker that she was sexually abused as a child and begins to cry uncontrollably," she said. "The worker, who was also sexually abused, feels overwhelmed with memories of her own abuse and discloses her abuse to the client. In this instance, her sharing was precipitated by her own emotional reaction and needs, not the client's." Martha went on. "Now suppose a caseworker, which in this case really could be you, Melissa, happens to be a former welfare recipient, and is listening to the story of a new client who is having trouble making ends meet. She decides to tell the client that success is possible because at one time she had relied on welfare and food stamps and was able to get back on her feet with the support she received. In this instance, the worker was not sharing to work out her own feelings but did so to help the client feel more hopeful about her ability to improve her situation. Do you see the difference?" she asked.

"I do," said David, "but it seems like that could be a very fine line to walk. Isn't it possible for the client to benefit even if the worker is doing it for his or her own reasons?"

"It is a fine line," Martha answered gently. "Part of it is the underlying motivation, but the bottom line is that true professionals need to know how to separate their own needs from the needs of the client."

Melissa had been listening to the give and take, but now spoke up. "We hear a lot about this issue in class, but the way you describe it really makes sense, Martha. It does make me feel a little better, but I still wonder sometimes what is okay to share with clients. In class I've heard students share lots of personal stories, and sometimes even my professors have shared things about themselves that were a bit surprising."

"Well," Martha answered, "it depends on what they're sharing and what their intent is. Some of my most memorable professors used personal stories about their families and their own backgrounds to illustrate points in class or teach techniques we could use. I remember one talking about her experience parenting a teenager that I've used not only with my clients but with my own kids. But in general, we shouldn't share personal information with clients if we're unsure of our motives. And then, if we do disclose something, it should be in very general terms, like saying 'I know how hard it is to balance work and school at the same time' or 'I remember my parents made me crazy when I was a teenager.' Just keep it general and focused on the client and be sure you are sharing because you think it will benefit the client."

Melissa listened as David added his thoughts on the subject. "So based on what you've said, Melissa probably could have explored the issue with her client today, since the client was clearly in distress about her situation and afraid of what would happen to her and her son. It might have helped her to know that Melissa had been there and was now doing well."

Martha nodded her head in agreement. "You're right, David." She turned to Melissa and said, "I'm glad you brought this up Melissa, especially in light of the increase in clients we're likely to see if we get this new grant. We see people with a multitude of problems and will most likely relate to some of them in personal ways. The fact that you're already thinking along these lines shows me you're on top of things."

The waitress came by to clear the table and a minute later Carlos arrived with three servings of *tres leches* cake, just as he had promised.

"Listen," Martha began as she savored the creamy dessert, "since we worked through dinner, why don't you come in a little later tomorrow? I'm going to a breakfast meeting with Ruth first thing in the morning, so we can all get together around ten or ten-thirty."

"That's cool with me," said David, finishing his last bite. "I'm not going to turn down the chance to sleep in!"

Questions for Discussion

1. Appointed by Franklin Delano Roosevelt to Secretary of Labor during the Great Depression, Frances Perkins, a social worker, was instrumental in implementing the first minimum wage law in 1938. Do you think a minimum wage standard is necessary? What arguments can be made for and against federal and state minimum wage standards?

2. The Fair Minimum Wage Act of 2007 raised the federal minimum wage in three 70-cent increments to $5.85 in July 2007, $6.55 in July 2008, and $7.25 in July 2009. Calculate the full-time annual income for each of these three wage levels. Next, using the cost-of-living in your community as a rough guide, discuss the challenges a family of two or three would likely face in meeting basic needs on these levels of income.

3. The Food Stamps Program (recently renamed the Supplemental Nutrition and Assistance Program, or SNAP) is operated by the Food and Nutrition Service of the U.S. Department of Agriculture. It serves over thirty million low-income people each month, yet, as the chapter noted, many eligible individuals and households do not claim the benefits to which they are

entitled. Why do you think some eligible recipients do not apply for food stamp benefits? What do you think can or should be done to improve the program's outreach?

4. The number of women with children in the paid labor force has significantly increased over the last thirty years. As a result, the cost and accessibility of childcare has become a considerable burden for many families, and has led many childcare advocates to say "Parents can't afford to pay, workers can't afford to stay, there's got to be a better way!" Do you think the government should be involved in providing and/or subsidizing childcare in the United States? Why or why not?

5. Helping Hands conducted a needs-assessment survey prior to formally preparing their grant proposal. What are the potential benefits of conducting a client needs assessment? What are the potential drawbacks?

6. A basic tenet of good social work practice is that planning occurs *with* clients, not for clients. What different types of methods can be used to conduct an informative assessment of client/consumer needs?

Innovative Assignments

1. The Helping Hands survey conducted by David and Melissa found that childcare costs and availability were major concerns for clients. What are the average costs in your community for full-time care of infants and preschool-aged children? Is center-based evening or weekend care available in your community? Is subsidized childcare available in your community? If so, how long are the waiting lists? What are the implications of your findings on low-income households with children?

2. It is important for students in human services to have personal experience with issues that affect low-income clients. Here are two components of an assignment that can give you a sense of that experience.
   Option 1: This option requires you to live within the budget and rules of the food stamp program for two weeks. Select a "typical" food stamp budget, then document and analyze your experience. In what ways did your shopping habits and diet change? Did you ever go hungry during your two-week trial? How easy or difficult would it be to rely on food stamps and abide by program rules while working?
   Option 2: This option requires you to keep a detailed accounting of your food purchases/expenses for two weeks. Examine and compare these purchases in light of food stamp budget allowances and regulations. How much did you spend on food purchases during the two-week period? What portion of your food purchases would not have been allowed under the rules of the food stamp program?

Both options are intended to familiarize you with the food stamp program and to demonstrate your knowledge of program strengths and weaknesses. Whatever option is chosen, the paper should include the following:

a. Identify which option you chose and explain why you chose it.
b. Demonstrate an awareness of the rules that apply to the food stamp program.
c. Provide information about what it takes to apply for and receive food stamps.
d. Describe an appropriate food stamp budget for your household and defend the appropriateness of the benefit level you have chosen.
e. Provide an analysis of the strengths and weaknesses of the program (conceptually and based on your experience) and recommendations to improve the program based on your analysis.
f. Clearly and accurately document your purchases during the two-week period.
g. Summarize your experience. Was it valuable? What was learned?

Suggested Readings

Barnett, W. S., & Ackerman, D. (2006). Costs, benefits, and long-term effects of early care and education programs: Recommendations and cautions for community developers. *Community Development, 37*, 86–100.

Bernstein, N. (2003, October 19). Daily choice turned deadly: Children left on their own. *The New York Times.* Available at http://www.nytimes.com/2003/10/19/nyregion/19MOTH.html

Capizzano, J., Adams, G., & Sonestein, F. (2000). *Child care arrangements for children under five: Variation across states. New federalism: National survey of America's families, Series B* (no. B-7). Washington, DC: The Urban Institute.

Clarke-Stewart, A., & Allhusen, V. (2005). *What we know about childcare.* Cambridge, MA: Harvard University Press.

Cnaan, R., & Boddie, S. (2002). Charitable choice and faith-based welfare: A call for social work. *Social Work, 47*(3), 224–235.

Gennetian, L. A., Crosby, D. A., Huston, A. C., & Lowe, E. D. (2004). Can child care assistance in welfare and employment programs support the employment of low-income families? *Journal of Policy Analysis and Management, 23*, 723–743.

Giannarelli, L., & Barsimantov, J. (2000). *Child care expenses of America's families.* Washington, DC: The Urban Institute.

Greenberg, A. (2000). Doing whose work? Faith-based organizations and government partnerships. In M. J. Bane, B. Coffin, & R. Thiemann (Eds.), *Who will provide? The changing role of religion in American social welfare* (pp. 178–97). Boulder, CO: Westview Press.

Handley, D. M. (2008). Strengthening the intergovernmental grant system: Long-term lessons for the federal & local relationship. *Public Administration Review, 68*(1), 126–136.

Hays, S. (2003). *Flat broke with children: Women in the age of welfare reform.* New York: Oxford University Press.

Kaushal, N. (2007). Welfare reform and family expenditures: How are single mothers adapting to the new welfare and work regime? *Social Service Review, 81*(3), 369–396.

Morgan, K. (2001). A child of the 60s: The great society, the new right, and the politics of federal child care. *Journal of Political History, 13*(2), 215–250.

Morrisey, T. (2008). Familial factors associated with the use of multiple child-care arrangements. *Journal of Marriage and Family, 70*(2), 549–563.

Ratcliffe, C., McKernan, S., & Finegold, K. (2007). *The effect of state food stamp and TANF policies on food stamp program participation.* Retrieved June 26, 2008, from http://www.urban.org/url.cfm?ID=411438

Rigby, E., Ryan, R., & Brooks-Gunn, J. (2007). Child care quality in different state policy contexts. *Journal of Policy Analysis and Management, 26*(4), 887–908.

Siegel, D., & Abbott, A. (2007). The work lives of the low-income welfare poor. *Families in Society, 88*(3), 401–412.

Stoeker, Randy. (2007). The research practices and needs of non-profit organizations in an urban center. *Journal of Sociology and Social Welfare, 34*(4), 97–119.

Wineburg, R., Coleman, B., Boddie, S., & Cnaan, R. (2008). Leveling the playing field: Devolution through faith-based organizations. *Journal of Sociology and Social Welfare, 35*(1), 17–42.

CHAPTER 3

Putting It All Together: Innovation, Flexibility, and Teamwork

JUNE 16, 2004

The next morning, Martha's head was still filled with the ideas she had discussed with David and Melissa afterhours and at dinner. Information from the surveys clearly demonstrated multiple employment-related challenges faced by those they hoped to serve with this new grant. Consequently, Martha was even more determined for Helping Hands to take the lead in organizing and eventually implementing a comprehensive welfare-to-work program.

Martha headed downtown to a Council of Community Services (CCS) meeting with Ruth, her lively social-service coordinator. The Council met each month in the local United Way office and provided social service agencies in the area the chance to share information about new programs and policies, discuss gaps in services for various populations, and network for potential partnerships. Martha faithfully attended these meetings, not only to hear the latest from her colleagues, but also to keep Helping Hands in the minds of other social service agencies. Martha knew the value of good PR. Last month the group had discussed implementing a model computer system that would track services given to individuals and households across agencies. The discussion had taken on a somewhat heated tone between those who supported the system as a way to minimize duplication of services and to determine how much and what types of assistance were being given to individuals and households and those who opposed it as an unneeded expense and another "big brother" mechanism that could be used against the low-income populations they served. Martha knew that the RFP from the Workforce Board would come up in this meeting and wanted to find out if other members of the consortium were planning to apply. She also wanted to follow-up with a few agencies that might be interested in forming a partnership with Helping Hands. The RFP had been very clear that programs were not merely to extend or duplicate existing efforts, and Martha wanted to be sure that the proposal Helping Hands submitted would fill a unique service niche in the community.

As she drove, Martha discussed the survey results with Ruth and recapped the previous day's discussions. "It's clear we have our work cut out for us," she said as she maneuvered in the heavy traffic toward a downtown exit.

Ruth wasted no time in adding her two cents. "You already know what I think," she exclaimed. "We need ESL classes. You know, when I moved from the Dominican Republic, we were fighting the War on Poverty and my whole family was able to take literacy classes. We even had a social worker who ran a program to help acculturate immigrants. We went to museums, theatrical shows, you name it," she recounted with her typical flourish.

"Really?" said Martha. In school she had heard her professors talk about how different it was working for community action agencies in the 1960s, but the idea of having program funds to take clients to cultural events ran against the current of personal responsibility evoked in the welfare reform act that President Clinton had signed into law eight years before. Her mind quickly raced to the possibility of including something similar in the grant application, perhaps as a reward for client participation or for achieving some important outcome, but Ruth brought her back to the discussion at hand.

"Yes, really!" she emphatically stated. "I remember she took me, my brothers and sisters, and other kids from the neighborhood for a guided tour of the central library. I'd never seen so many books. I like that place so much I just took Linda and Melissa to see *The Day After Tomorrow* because the library is in the film. It was great."

"The twins went the day it opened," Martha replied, returning from her brief reverie, "and lord knows it's been hot enough these last few days to make me believe in global warming!" She exited the freeway and turned toward downtown. The sun was gleaming brilliantly against the window facades of the buildings.

"Back in my day, we would have opened up a fire hydrant and cooled off right there in the street," said Ruth. "But they won't let the kids do that anymore."

"Well, we do have a river," Martha playfully noted.

"*En una manera, es la misma cosa,*" Ruth blurted with a degree of frustration. "It's the same thing. When I came here, people believed that the government could really help. Now poor people, especially immigrants, are viewed as the problem, and the government's job is to limit the resources available to *los pobres.*" Ruth had a unique way of mixing Spanish and English, but somehow Martha always seemed to understand what she was saying.

"How else can you explain tax cuts for the rich and time limits for single mothers on welfare?" Ruth rhetorically questioned, shaking her head.

Martha nodded but was too busy navigating the one-way downtown streets to respond.

"*Fíjate,*" Ruth continued, "nothing is more fundamental for many of our clients than being able to speak and write English, but classes can be expensive, inconvenient, and inaccessible. Without language skills they'll be stuck in low-paying jobs forever. A couple of agencies in town provide classes, but there aren't enough being offered, not in our area anyway."

"Well, partnerships were mentioned in the RFP," Martha replied, referring to the subject that had just been occupying her thoughts. She turned in to the parking lot of the United Way building and looked for a spot in the shade. "While we're here, let's keep our eyes open for potential partners."

During the CCS meeting, Martha learned that several agencies had plans to apply for the welfare-to-work funds, but more importantly, she spotted Leticia Soto, Executive Director of the Literacy Initiative, an adult basic education and English as a Second Language (ESL) provider. She and Ruth made an appointment with Leticia for later in the week to discuss a partnership for the grant.

A representative from the Workforce Board was present at the meeting, and Martha was impressed to hear that bidders meetings and conference calls would be conducted all over the state to answer questions about the application process. She learned that the Workforce Board planned to fund at least one program in each region of the state, but that there was no limit to the number of programs that could be funded in each region. The presenter noted that the governor was keeping an eye on the process and at a recent prayer luncheon had publicly indicated that he hoped to see a strong showing of applications from faith-based organizations (FBOs). "Charitable Choice is back in the limelight" thought Martha upon hearing of the governor's interest. Charitable Choice was a controversial provision in the 1996 welfare reform law that sought to increase the presence of faith-based organizations in the delivery of welfare services, but not much had changed in River City in the years since its passage. Even when President Bush set up the Office of Faith-Based and Community Initiatives shortly after assuming office, the tax-exempt arms of long-standing faith-based groups like Catholic Charities, Lutheran Social Services, and the Salvation Army continued to lead community faith-based social service efforts. It certainly wasn't individual churches or congregations of any faith. But perhaps this was about to change.

After the meeting, Martha and Ruth returned to the office and, after a quick lunch, convened with David and Linda to discuss what they had learned at the meeting and review the needs-assessment data. Ruth brought along a bag of cookies.

"These are good," said Linda, "but not as good as the *tres leches* cake David was telling me about! I should have worked late last night," she said smiling.

"Don't worry, Linda," Martha responded, "I'm always looking for a good reason to go to Carlos' restaurant!"

"Besides," David quickly interjected, "you got to go to a movie last week!"

"I think we're spoiling them," Ruth said, looking at Martha in mock disapproval. Martha knew that the salaries she was able to offer her staff were limited, and though it was sometimes a financial stretch, she enjoyed spoiling them from time to time, especially when they did such good work. As her staff munched on the cookies, Martha decided to get the meeting back on track.

"I've heard from David, Ruth, and Melissa about the survey," Martha said, "but do you have any thoughts, Linda?"

"As a matter of fact, I do," she replied. "I was surprised at how many respondents are employed, just not full time. I don't know if this means that full-time jobs are hard to come by, or if they are not qualified or able to get the full-time jobs that are available."

"Probably some mix of both," David interjected. "Or maybe it's the whole childcare thing again." The others nodded.

"Also," Linda added, "this isn't a survey result, per se, but just this morning a client was explaining to me how time consuming it is to go from agency to agency to get help with small amounts of money for rent and utility assistance. Maybe we could offer more than we are able to offer now," she said in a half-questioning tone.

Martha listened to what Linda had to say. A bigger picture was forming in her mind of how the program they designed should look. It should involve partnerships, she thought, and take care of important short-term needs while not losing sight of the potential for long-term change through some sort of employment-related training.

As if reading Martha's mind, Ruth reiterated her desire to include ESL training as part of the program. "I know our clients have a lot of emergency needs," she began, "but I think we need to include literacy training if we are going to truly help people move out of poverty. Otherwise we run the risk of just putting band-aids on the situation." Everyone seemed to agree.

Martha knew that the problems her clients faced were not just short-term in nature, and often interconnected. Despite the "work first" mantra that followed in the wake of welfare reform, she knew that simply finding a job wasn't enough. She remembered a book she had read titled *Making Ends Meet*. The authors had shown that single mothers in low-wage jobs faced personal and financial hardships that were often worse than women relying on welfare, yet the sign she had seen hanging in a local welfare office—A JOB, A BETTER JOB, A CAREER—made it seem so straightforward. She knew it would not be easy to make this a reality for low-income households facing multiple employment barriers, but the more she thought of it, the more she liked the opportunity the Workforce Board grant represented and the ideas that she and her staff were generating. She was eager to start putting together a program that would support a solid ensemble of services for low-income families seeking to become economically self-sufficient.

On Friday, Martha and Julia participated in a conference call with regional representatives from the Workforce Board. Agency representatives from River City and surrounding counties who were interested in applying for funding also participated. "Competition is going to be stiff," Martha thought as she listened to the Workforce Board representatives address questions about eligibility criteria, budget requirements, service options and delivery, and collaborations between agencies. Not surprisingly, the majority of questions focused on the types of services that the Workforce Board would consider as meeting the welfare-to-work criteria. Martha was surprised when an affirmative response was given to a caller who asked if paying for tattoo removal would be considered a legitimate welfare-to-work service. It appeared that the Workforce Board would be willing to accept some creative proposals as long as a strong argument could be made for their efficacy.

By the end of the call, two things were apparent: First, Dr. Gault was right. The Workforce Board representative indicated that the programs would be evaluated by an outside organization, and that programs receiving funding would be required to fully cooperate with the evaluators. Second, it was clear that organizing and funding the welfare-to-work grants was a new process for the Workforce Board. This was definitely not going to be a business-as-usual arrangement. The representative had even said that the Workforce Board was not looking at this as just another way of disbursing welfare funds, but as a way to partner with local community-based organizations to promote community development. Martha had never heard the Workforce Board use such language, but had to admit that the phone conference had been very informative. She now had a much better idea of what the Workforce Board was looking for, but still worried about the limited time that was available to put together a solid application.

On Monday morning, Martha called Reverend William Anderson, the lead pastor of a large congregation and the chair of an ecumenical council that organized social services among a small number of participating churches. Information she had obtained at the CCS meeting and the conference call made it clear that having a faith-based organization as part of the collaboration she was assembling would most likely strengthen the appeal of the application. She was also very familiar with the childcare services that Rev. Anderson's church provided. Her children had participated in an after-school program there years before when Rev. Anderson had been the youth pastor.

"Good morning, Reverend, this is Martha from Helping Hands."

"Martha, it's good to hear from you!" Rev. Anderson replied. "How are you doing? And the twins?"

"We're all doing well, thank you Reverend."

"And how are your godparents doing these days?" Rev. Anderson had officiated at her godparents' fiftieth wedding anniversary celebration a few months earlier.

"They're doing just fine, Reverend, though Uncle Henry complains that he's getting too old to tend his garden like he should."

"Just as long as he can still make it to services on Sunday," Rev. Anderson quipped with a laugh. "So how can I help you, Martha?"

"Reverend, I'm wondering if you would be interested in working with my agency to provide services for low-income families." Martha wasted no time ascertaining if Rev. Anderson would be interested in partnering with Helping Hands.

"Martha, if you have something that will be of benefit to my flock, then I'm all ears!" he replied. Rev. Anderson was a charismatic ecclesiastical leader and frequently referred members of his congregation to Martha's organization when he didn't have the resources to help them himself.

"Actually, Reverend, I'm talking about an opportunity for the entire community."

"Martha! Everyone in this community is a member of my flock, some just don't know it yet!" he laughed. Rev. Anderson's sense of humor won hearts wherever he went. Martha knew there were two components of a welfare-to-work program that Helping Hands could not provide without community partners: literacy training classes and childcare. She broached the subject with Rev. Anderson. After they chatted for a few minutes, they agreed it would be better to talk in person, so they arranged to meet at Rev. Anderson's church the following afternoon.

As Martha hung up the phone, Julia popped her head in the office door.

"Evy has been asking about the proposal budget," she said, "but I still don't know how much we are going to ask for."

Julia had been working hard gathering information for the grant proposal and had put together some charts documenting the number of clients Helping Hands had served over the last three-month period and the average amount of rent and utility assistance the clients had received.

"That's a good question," Martha replied. "I just got off the phone with Rev. Anderson, and I think he's interested in being a part of this. If we're going to offer childcare, in whatever form, it's going to be expensive. Why don't we start with the maximum, and work back from that. We can always cut back if we can't defend asking for that much."

"So . . . , five hundred thousand dollars for the two-year cycle? That would just about double our budget!" Julia said excitedly.

"I know," said Martha, nodding her head. "During the phone conference, one of the callers asked if lower-budget applications would be looked at more favorably. The rep from the Workforce Board said that all that mattered was that the budget be appropriately justified. If the goal of this grant is to make a real difference in people's lives, well, that just can't be done on the cheap. Like Ruth says, we should do more than . . ."

". . . just put band-aids on people's problems," Julia finished, smiling. One good thing about Ruth was that no one had to guess where she stood on the issues.

"I'm going to discuss the possibilities with Rev. Anderson in more detail tomorrow afternoon," Martha explained, "and while I don't want to get to far ahead of things, with a little luck, I should have some preliminary numbers for you soon on the childcare component."

"It's due in less than two weeks," said Julia, "but I'll let Evy know you're getting your ducks in a row."

The following day Rev. Anderson greeted Martha in the lobby of his church office. He joked with Martha as they made their way to his office where he sank into a large chair behind a desk covered with papers.

"As you can see, Martha, I've already got more paperwork than I can handle!" the Reverend chuckled.

"Well you're in luck, Reverend," Martha said with a smile. "As the lead contract agency, Helping Hands will take care of all the reporting requirements for this grant. We're just looking for your church to provide some childcare, probably after hours and maybe on Saturdays while we offer literacy classes as part of the special welfare-to-work program we hope to get."

"Well, that answers my big question, because we don't have any extra daytime slots available right now," he said, leaning back in his chair. "We take care of about fifty kids, most of them on a sliding scale. So you're talking about extending the childcare to encompass some evenings and weekends, right?"

"That's it," Martha replied.

"We can't do Wednesday nights," said Rev. Anderson, shaking his head. "That's bible-study night."

Martha smiled and maintained her composure.

"Yes, of course, Reverend," she answered calmly. "I guess it depends on how many people end up taking the classes, but just to be clear, you would be able to offer childcare on weekday evenings other than Wednesdays?"

"Timewise, I don't think that would be a problem," said Rev. Anderson as he leaned further back in his chair and put his hands behind his head. "But where are the classes going to be held? What about staff? Is there money in this grant to hire childcare workers, or are we talking about using volunteers?"

Martha felt herself relax a bit. Rev. Anderson's questions were cautious but hopeful. "Finding volunteers for those hours might be a bit of a challenge," he added.

"Since we're so close, the classes will be held at Helping Hands," Martha replied. And funds from the grant can be used to pay for childcare providers."

"I tell you what," Rev. Anderson countered, suddenly sitting up straight in his chair. "I have members of my congregation who are trying to turn their lives around. If you could help folks get their GED as part of your program, I'll throw in the church's van to shuttle the kids to and from our daycare center, *and* I'll have a hot meal waiting for them when they get here. You know the Good Lord didn't like his flock going hungry!"

Martha was surprised. She knew Rev. Anderson had charisma and a sense of humor, but she was finding out that he was also a savvy advocate. She also knew that the in-kind donations he offered added value to the program and represented the extra touch that the "armies of compassion" were able to offer.

"I'm pretty sure we can accommodate your request, Reverend," she said with a smile on her face. "We have a small computer room that would probably work out just fine, and I can't think of anyone better to provide GED assistance than Ruth, our services coordinator."

Rev. Anderson came around the desk, grabbed her hand in a hearty shake and replied, "Okay, Martha! Let's see what the heavens will bring!"

On the short trip back to her office, Martha breathed a sigh of relief. The first step in the process had gone as smoothly as she could have expected.

The next day, Martha and Ruth grabbed a quick bite to eat on their way to the appointment they had made earlier with Leticia Soto, the Executive Director of the Literacy Initiative. The tiny corner market where they stopped to pick up sandwiches was covered in graffiti, and the counter inside where they ordered was shielded behind a plate of bullet-proof glass. Martha was again reminded of how much things had changed in her old neighborhood. Getting back in the sweltering car, she remembered making trips here as a girl, when it was a friendly mom-and-pop store with an honest-to-goodness, old-fashioned soda fountain. It saddened Martha to see how the area had deteriorated.

As Ruth drove, Martha looked over an outline of a tentative proposal they had put together. Martha wanted to make sure she used a positive approach that would open the door to a productive partnership.

"You ready?" said Ruth, as she parked the car and turned off the air conditioning. Martha slid the paper into her briefcase and opened the door. A blast of hot air hit her face.

"Remind me to make more morning appointments," she joked to Ruth on their way in.

Martha and Ruth stepped into a brightly colored lobby and were greeted warmly by the receptionist. "Hola," Ruth said in reply. "Tenemos una cita con Leticia a la una."

"Momentito, por favor," the receptionist said as she motioned for them to have a seat.

Some of the bilingual posters hanging in the lobby notifying clients of the Women, Infants, and Children (WIC) program and the Children's Health Care Initiative (CHIP) were also hanging on the walls inside Helping Hands. Martha took that as a good sign. An older poster of César Chávez, with the caption Sí Se Puede, hung in the corner. In a few minutes Leticia came bursting gregariously through the door.

"Ladies, buenas tardes! So happy to see you. Come on back to my office, and let's figure out what we can do with this grant proposal." Leticia and Ruth chatted in Spanish as she led them through a winding hall to her office.

"Leticia, I am so glad you're excited about this funding opportunity," Martha exclaimed, feeling that she wouldn't have to make much of a sales pitch. "Let's jump right into it. Basically, we're hoping to partner with the Literacy Initiative to offer ESL classes at our agency."

An unexpectedly cloudy look came over Leticia's face. "Listen, we would love to be able to offer more classes on the west side. But unfortunately, I don't think this grant will allow us to do that."

"Why not?" asked Ruth, clearly upset that her idea was being nullified before it had received a fair hearing.

"We've already looked into it," Leticia replied. "But it seems that the Workforce Board is adhering to some serious immigration restrictions. Participants have to be U.S. citizens or residents who have been here since the welfare reform act was passed in nineteen ninety-six.

"You've got to be kidding!" Ruth gasped, incredulously.

"I wish I was," Leticia responded flatly. "But they're not going to budge. And it doesn't make much sense to offer classes to folks who have been here for eight or more years. We just wouldn't have the numbers," she added, shrugging her shoulders.

It was clear that Leticia had been through the ringer in her efforts to help immigrants while dealing with government bureaucracies and an increasingly hostile citizenry.

"Why didn't this come up at the CCS meeting or the bidders' conference?" Martha asked.

Leticia nodded her head in understanding. "I think the focus was on the budget, the services that would be allowed, and meeting the income eligibility requirements. And frankly, I think the Workforce Board is still ironing out the wrinkles themselves."

Martha certainly shared her feelings on this point.

"All the legal documentation the grant requires would have been problematic anyway," Leticia added in a resigned tone.

Ruth folded her arms across her chest, a gesture that did nothing to hide her disappointment, while Martha mentally searched for some other angle that might be pursued with the Literacy Initiative. Leticia broke the momentary silence.

"I do have another idea," she offered tentatively.

"¡Bueno pues, porque yo no tengo nada!" Ruth blurted in frustration, waving her hand dismissively.

"No tengo nada" (I have nothing). Though Martha's Spanish was limited, she had recently overheard a Spanish-speaking client utter those same words to Ruth during an interview.

Leticia continued. "I've had a number of my ESL students take a class offered at River City CC to become Certified Nursing Assistants. It's really a good opportunity. The classes are short, relatively affordable, and there's demand for full-time CNAs in local nursing facilities and health care agencies."

Leticia could see that she had Martha and Ruth's attention.

"Anyway," she continued, "a few of my students have struggled with completing the CNA course, some due to their lack of fluency, but most of them for other reasons . . ."

"Like what?" interrupted Ruth, intrigued.

"A lot of them have limited schooling or they've been out of school for years; either way they're not ready for the medical lingo, and they need better study habits. Some of them can't afford the fees and equipment that are required; others just can't balance all their responsibilities, especially child-care. Another problem is that students are not allowed to miss one class over the three-week session. If they do, they're dropped from the program."

"That seems a bit harsh," interjected Martha.

"That's the rule," Leticia stated flatly. "I think they could really use some sort of class that would help prepare them for the CNA course, you know? I'd do it if I could, but we're swamped already."

Although disappointed about her original plans being shot down, Ruth saw potential in this new opportunity.

"If I could sit in on this class, Martha, I'm sure I could come up with a curriculum for a prep course."

Martha smiled at Ruth's enthusiasm. A moment ago her arms were crossed in frustration; now she was proposing to devise and teach a course on an entirely new subject. But if anybody could do it, it would be Ruth.

"I have no doubt you could," Martha said definitively. She pondered the situation for a minute then added, "And I don't think it would change things from the childcare standpoint." The more she thought about it, childcare would be an essential element to any training they could offer. "In fact, it sounds like childcare is a key ingredient to helping students get through the CNA course." The wheels were turning in Martha's head. "Leticia," she asked, "do you have a daily paper?"

Leticia looked in a basket of recycled paper. "I have yesterday's" she said, somewhat confused at Martha's request.

"That'll do," responded Martha as she took the paper and thumbed through it hastily. Leticia shot Ruth a quizzical glance but received a calm look in return. Ruth had worked with Martha too long not to trust what she was doing. Martha identified the section she was looking for and quickly folded the paper in two to get a better look.

"That's what I was hoping for!" she said as she pointed to a particular section. "There are six full-time certified nursing assistant positions advertised in the paper," she explained, "and the beginning salaries that are listed are all well over the minimum wage."

"That's not saying much," said Ruth, in obvious reference to her dissatisfaction with the $5.15 federal minimum that would still leave a two-person family with a full-time worker in poverty.

"Well, it's a start," responded Martha. "What do you think, Leticia?" she asked.

"Honestly?" Leticia replied, "I think it's the best opportunity going with just short-term training. There are openings for childcare workers, but they don't make as much, and CNAs have more career advancement potential."

Martha, Leticia, and Ruth looked at each other and thought about the new direction the proposal had taken. Then a smile crossed Martha's face.

"I think our application to the Workforce Board just got a little more interesting!" she said enthusiastically. "But this puts a lot of responsibility on you, Ruth. Are you up for it?"

"¿Está en serio?" Ruth responded with an air of feigned indignity. "After teaching in New York City for twenty years, I can do anything!" she laughed.

Later that afternoon, Martha and Ruth contacted Carol Simpson, the lead instructor for the CNA program at River City Community College, and shared their plans about developing a prep course and providing ancillary support that would help students be better prepared to succeed in the course Carol taught. Carol was thrilled at the prospect and invited Ruth to sit through the next three-week course session, which thankfully took place on Tuesday and Thursday nights. She also offered to provide referrals for students who met the eligibility requirements and needed additional assistance. Martha liked the fact that RCCC would act as an informal partner in the welfare-to-work project and would not have to be listed as a formal subcontractor in the application to the Workforce Board. It would make the reporting and accounting requirements that much easier, and obviously help with recruitment.

Friday morning was the final staff meeting before the proposal was due. Julia made sure there was plenty of coffee, and everyone was ready to piece together the final components of the grant.

"Okay, everybody, here's what we are going to put in this grant proposal," Martha began. "We will provide a combination of services. Helping Hands will serve as the lead agency, providing emergency financial assistance to eligible clients. We will pay for things like rent, utilities, bus passes, gas vouchers, car repair, workforce related clothing, and fees for tests and licenses. In addition to the financial assistance, we will also be holding CNA prep classes here at our agency two nights a week. Each prep course will last three weeks, just like the CNA courses. Individuals attending these classes will be eligible to receive additional financial assistance to help purchase books, uniforms, and other essentials. The classes will be taught in our meeting room by Ruth, our resident teacher extraordinaire."

Ruth took a bow and received some applause from the group.

Martha continued. "Finally, in exchange for some GED tutorials, Reverend Anderson's church has agreed to provide childcare during the hours that classes are taught."

"And don't forget, a hot meal too!" Julia added.

The staff agreed that this seemed like an effective combination of services. The proposal incorporated many of the elements in the guidelines set forth in the RFP. It was a collaboration between community- and faith-based service providers, it offered training for employment that was otherwise not available, it targeted groups that had multiple employment barriers, and the services supported the overall goal of workforce preparation and welfare avoidance. Everyone hoped it would get the Workforce Board's attention.

"This may sound crazy," said Melissa in youthful exuberation, "but I feel like I'm already connected to this new program. If our proposal isn't selected, I'm going to be crushed!"

A veteran of the grant-funding game, Martha knew that it was never wise to pin one's hopes on a single funding source or think that a grant was in the bag, but she also knew where Melissa was coming from. Her staff had put in a great deal of time and energy to make this a first-rate proposal.

"Let's just keep thinking positively, okay?" Martha responded. "Julia, Ruth, and I are going to finish writing the grant over the weekend so it will be ready for the board to review on Monday," Martha explained. "I want to thank all of you for your input and diligent work these past few weeks. This has definitely been a team effort, and I'm excited to see where it takes us. If we're successful, we may be able to create some pretty important changes in the community for our clients."

At the noon board meeting on Monday, Martha was tired but full of anticipation as she greeted each board member. She felt a twinge of guilty relief when it became clear that Ronald Tripp was the only board member who could not attend. Nevertheless, she made a mental note to send him an electronic copy of the proposal and give him a chance to provide input. Julia had placed a copy of the grant proposal in front of each chair in the conference room, and with a minimum of their usual greetings and conversation, the board members began to scrutinize the proposal. As soon as the last board member had finished, Martha moved to the head of the conference table and began the meeting.

"Thank you for coming in today. Rather than spending a lot of time on formalities, I'd like to get right to the heart of the matter. We've spent the last two weeks working with Reverend Anderson's church and the lead instructor of the certified nursing assistant program at city community—you see them mentioned in the proposal—to put together what we think is an extensive welfare-to-work program that will enable our clients to overcome emergency financial problems and find and maintain employment."

Martha was glad that she had contacted the board members earlier and notified them of their intention to teach a CNA prep course rather than ESL classes. Despite the old saying "It is easier to say your sorry than to ask for permission," Martha knew that giving the board a heads-up on the change would be for the best. She turned to the easel behind her and picked up a marker.

"Our goal is simple. First, we want to provide emergency financial assistance that will help our clients overcome financial barriers to employment. The rent and utility assistance is meant to provide our clients with a basic level of housing security. As Dr. Gault has noted on many occasions, we want to help our clients avoid the downward spiral that can come with eviction and utility cutoffs. We also plan to offer transportation assistance in the form of bus passes, gas vouchers, and even car repair if that is what would help clients the most. And as I discussed with each of you, we believe the CNA prep classes will help students to successfully complete the CNA class offered at city community. Ruth has agreed to teach the classes if the grant is approved. Finally, Reverend Anderson has agreed to provide childcare for our clients' children when they take both the prep course and the course at city community."

Martha surveyed the room, trying to gauge each board member's reaction to the proposal.

Professor Gault was the first to speak. "Martha, I really like what you have done with this proposal. I'm just concerned about the childcare component." He shifted in his seat, leaning forward toward the table.

"I think it's great that we want to provide childcare for the CNA students, but childcare is such a pressing need, shouldn't we offer it to all of the welfare-to-work clients who may need it?"

"We had thought about including full-time childcare in the proposal," Martha responded, "but once we ran the numbers, it was so expensive that we wouldn't have been able to offer any of the other services."

Julia quickly jumped in. "We even thought we might be able to trim it down a bit by paying for childcare only for those families that were on a government waiting list, but even that was too expensive."

Ever the businesswoman, Carlene suggested a compromise. "The good professor is right; childcare is a huge issue. But I also know a thing or two about bottom lines. What good is it going to do if students pass the courses, get their licenses, and then can't afford childcare? Could we offer childcare to those students who complete the courses and find jobs?"

Carlos raised a question. "Is there enough financial room to play with in this grant to provide full-time childcare to everyone who finishes the CNA program?"

"I hadn't thought of this before, but it may be possible, perhaps for a limited time. Say three to six months or so. We'd have to check the numbers," Martha speculated.

"It would certainly provide a healthy incentive for CNA students to stick with the program," added Professor Gault. The rest of the board members nodded their heads in agreement.

Dr. Shearer, examining a copy of the RFP closely, added her opinion to the discussion. "The RFP says that postemployment services are encouraged. I think if we couch childcare as a postemployment support, it would fit really well with what they are looking for."

"Sounds like this would be a popular move," said Carlene.

"Okay, then are we in agreement to move some money out of the financial assistance budget and place it in a new postemployment childcare category?" asked Carlos. The other board members nodded in agreement.

"If that's what you think is best," Martha said looking around the room, "then that's what we'll do! But unfortunately, Reverend Anderson doesn't have anymore room in his regular day program," she said with a note of resignation.

"Some sort of a voucher system would probably work best anyway," said Dr. Gault. "It would allow the CNA graduates to use it anywhere they like. All we need are the numbers."

Martha shot Julia a quick glance.

"I'll go get my calculator," Julia replied. "I could probably come up with a range of estimates in just a few minutes."

Martha couldn't believe that they had made a significant change to the proposal in such a smooth fashion. A few other small items in the budget were clarified, until only one more problem needed to be addressed.

"I thought we were going to have our next lunch meeting at Carlos' place," said Carlene in semiserious frustration. "Now I don't even see a box lunch sitting around!"

"Señora!" Carlos proclaimed. "Thank you for remembering! I have directed my wait staff to bring *comida* from Casa Yucateca at twelve-thirty. I didn't want to mix business with pleasure. A fine meal should be enjoyed, eh?"

Carlene got up from the table and gave Carlos a big hug.

By the next morning, Martha had put together the final components of the grant. She had Melissa make copies for the Workforce Board, and gathered the staff around to tell them how much she appreciated their effort.

"I want to thank all of you for your hard work these past three weeks," Martha said as she dramatically placed the completed proposal in a large envelope.

"Can I have the honor of stamping it and putting it in the mailbox?" asked David.

"Sorry, David," Martha said shaking her head in an exaggerated fashion, "but I'm taking this envelope to the Workforce Board myself!"

Five weeks later, Martha rushed in from a hurried lunch and headed to her desk. She had a number of client appointments and was running behind schedule. The number of clients Helping Hands served had increased recently due to the closing of a local manufacturing plant. Martha was picking up the slack in order to help as many clients as quickly as possible, but she was on edge, thinking about their dwindling resources. She put her purse into the file drawer and quickly listened to her phone messages, assessing the amount of time she was going to need for callbacks.

She was about to head to the lobby when Julia appeared at the door.

"Martha! There's a call from the Workforce Board, can I ring them through?" Julia had a look of calm in her eyes that belied her excitement.

"Absolutely! I'm ready . . . yes, I'm ready, let's see what they have to say," Martha replied, trying to play down her own excitement as she returned to her desk.

Julia forwarded the call and then returned in time to see Martha pick up the phone. She stood at the door while Martha quietly spoke to the caller. Martha's expression was calm and without a hint of what had just transpired.

"Well?" Julia's eyes grew wide as Martha slowly grinned.

"Well . . . we're in business! The Workforce Board was impressed with, and I quote, 'every facet of our proposal!' Call in the staff, and let's break the news!"

Questions for Discussion

1. Chapter 3 begins with Martha and Ruth attending their local Council of Community Services (CCS) meeting. Such councils operate in communities across the United States, and the issue of tracking service delivery to clients across agencies in those communities is a frequent topic of discussion for these groups. What are the pros and cons of establishing a tracking system to monitor client use of services across a community?

2. Faith-based agencies, such as Lutheran Social Services, Catholic Charities, and the Salvation Army, have been providing social services for many years, but under President Bush, an effort was made to encourage the faith community to take a broader role in social service delivery. (To some extent, these efforts have been continued under the Obama administration.) What are the strengths of using faith-based organizations in the delivery of social services to clients? What concerns could be raised about utilizing these entities for social service delivery?

3. Ruth referred to the War on Poverty, a series of programs and policies started during the administration of President Lyndon B. Johnson as part of the Economic Opportunity Act of 1964. What reasons do you think led President Johnson to mount such an aggressive offensive against poverty in the 1960s? Do you think another American president will seek to wage a campaign against poverty in the future? Why or why not?

4. In the 1990s, welfare reform abolished the long-standing Aid to Families with Dependent Children (AFDC) program and established Temporary Assistance for Needy Families, or TANF. The 1990s welfare reform also famously "devolved" welfare from federal to state and local authority, in essence allowing each state to set up key features of its own program. What are the pros and cons of emphasizing state and local control of welfare initiatives?

5. Do you think the assistance and services put together as part of Helping Hands' grant proposal is a good use of taxpayer money? Why or why not? What additional services or resources would you include to promote economic self-sufficiency among the low-income clients that Helping Hands serves?

Innovative Assignments

1. Research your local community's social services council or board, if one exists. Answer the following questions in your research. What is its mission? What agencies participate in the group? Is there a broad representation in terms of the types of clients they serve? How often and where do they meet and what are the foci of those meetings? Do they have officers, and if so, how are they chosen? What are some of the agency's recent projects or accomplishments?

2. Faith-based organizations such as Catholic Charities, are long-standing and well-known social service providers. As partners with state or local government, however, many churches or congregations are new to the field, and there are mixed reviews about their participation and performance in the social service arena. Contact the government office in your state that oversees faith-based initiatives to determine both the participation level and the overall performance of those programs. Are faith-based organizations actively participating in welfare-to-work or other antipoverty programs? In what other areas of social service delivery are they active? Have formal evaluations of these programs been published? What are the major findings?

Suggested Readings

Bane, M. J. (1997, January-February). Welfare as we might know it. *American Prospect*, 30, 47–53.

Clerkin, R. M., & Grønbjerg, K. A. (2007). The capacities and challenges of faith-based human service organizations. *Public Administration Review*, 67(1), 115–126.

Cnaan, R. (1999). *The newer deal: Social work and religion in partnership*. New York: Columbia University Press.

Edin, K., & Lein, L. (1997). *Making ends meet: How single mothers survive welfare and low-wage work*. New York: Russell Sage Foundation.

Gazley, B. (2008). Beyond the contract: The scope and nature of informal government & nonprofit partnerships. *Public Administration Review*, 68(1), 141–154.

Green, J. C., & Sherman, A. L. (2000). *Fruitful collaborations: A survey of government-funded faith-based programs in fifteen states*. Charlottesville, VA: Hudson Institute.

Kissane, R. J. (2006, June). Responsible but uninformed? Nonprofit and executive directors' knowledge of welfare reform. *Social Service Review*, 80(2),322–345.

Silverman, R. M. (2002). Vying for the urban poor: Charitable organizations, faith-based social capital, and racial reconciliation in a deep south city. *Sociological Inquiry*, 72(1), 151–165.

Smith, S. R., & Sosin, S. R. (2001). The varieties of faith-related agencies. *Public Administration Review*, 61(6), 651–670.

CHAPTER 4

A New Era Begins

OCTOBER 2004

Martha laid her pencil on the desk and breathed a deep sigh. She was heading into a meeting with her staff, Rev. Anderson, and Carol Simpson, the coordinator of the CNA program at River City Community College. Although Carol wasn't a paid partner on this grant, her assistance in getting clients into the prep course was crucial for Helping Hands. Thankfully, Carol was an enthusiastic supporter of the prep course and knew her students could truly benefit from the curriculum Ruth had put together. Martha was looking forward to sharing with the group how the various pieces of the program would work together and prepare them for the reimbursement and data collection required by the grant.

Martha walked into the conference room and found everyone waiting for her to start the meeting. The excitement in the room was evident. Ruth and Carol were animatedly chatting about the CNA program, and Rev. Anderson, with his typical flair, was regaling Linda, Melissa, Evy, and David with stories about the youngsters in the daycare at his church.

"...I actually caught the little rascal trying to bury one of my bibles!" he said, which elicited a peal of laughter from the group.

Martha was glad that the mood was so upbeat. She made some brief introductions and thanked the group for all their hard work in putting together a funded proposal. She then explained that they would begin the meeting with an overview of all aspects of the new program and end with a discussion of the billing and reporting requirements of the grant.

"But first," Martha began, with a hint of mischief behind her voice, I think Reverend Anderson has some news to share with us."

Rev. Anderson sat up in his chair and straightened his coat with dramatic effect. "No big deal!" he said, clearly playing the moment for everything it was worth. "Just ol' Willie and the governor having a private meeting, that's all!"

"What?" said the assembled group, laughing at the ostentatious manner that Rev. Anderson was putting on.

"What Reverend Anderson means to say," interjected Martha with a tone of teasing sincerity, "is that the governor has invited him and all the other faith-based welfare-to-work providers to the capitol next week for a press conference and a private meeting."

"Really? ¿De veras?" asked Ruth, obviously excited that the program was already receiving so much attention.

"That's right," said Rev. Anderson. "An all-expense-paid trip to the capitol to let Reverend Willie speak a little truth to power!" he exclaimed. It was certainly an exciting way to get the program started.

Getting back to business, Martha asked Ruth to share her experience in taking the CNA course, which she had just completed. Ruth could barely contain her enthusiasm as she explained how valuable this education could be for their clients. Always the teacher, Ruth passed out a brief outline of the CNA prep course she had developed. Carol followed with a copy of the requirements for her program, and thanked Helping Hands for including her in the planning and implementation of the prep course. Clearly, she and Ruth were already working well together. Martha reminded the staff that in additon to the prep course, the program would provide rental and utility assistance as well as childcare during the course and the actual CNA class. And as an incentive, Helping Hands would also pay for the clothing, equipment, and books necessary to take the CNA course for all those who passed Ruth's prep course. Finally, she emphasized that only those clients who passed the CNA course would be eligible for six months of assistance with childcare.

Martha then asked Evy to share what she'd developed for the billing and payment process. Evy reached into her satchel and brought out a handful of papers.

"I've brought copies of the forms for reimbursement. This grant only pays us after services have been rendered and reported. Most state grants work this way, but there are some now that are performance based. In that type of contract, the state not only won't pay until services have been delivered, but also won't pay unless the agency achieves certain outcomes for clients as agreed upon in the contract. I'm really glad this contract is not funded that way."

Evy went on to detail the billing process itself. "This applies to Reverend Anderson," she stated, "as his church is our only subcontractor." She explained that Helping Hands would need the billing for a previous month's work on the fifteenth day of the following month in order to process payment by the first day of the month after that.

"Basically, it works like this: you provide services in January, for which you will bill us on the fifteenth of February. We will then process your billing and have a check to you by the first day of March, if all goes well and we don't hit any snags. It could be later in the month, but we're going to do our best to meet that first day mark."

Evy explained that payment for expenses related to the CNA course would be paid once the agency received a bill from the community college for qualified clients. "As Carol knows, we've set up a third-party payer system with RCCC. That means the students use Helping Hands as a source of financial aid, just like they would a loan or grant program. The college just bills us directly rather than billing the students," she said.

Melissa spoke up. "As the only student here, I can tell you that I always worry about financial aid coming through each semester. I think it will be a huge relief for the clients to know we're covering this for them."

Evy continued. "Carol, we'll need you to send a separate bill for each student. Once we've confirmed that they've registered for your course, we'll go ahead and pay for the other things that they'll need."

Rev. Anderson sat quietly while Evy shared this new information. His mood had changed from the beginning of the meeting, and now he looked visibly concerned. He leaned back in his chair and rubbed his balding head.

"Martha, I don't know if we can wait this long on my end to get paid. We're a church; we've got limited funds and have to pay our bills just like everybody else. I knew we'd have to bill you, but I didn't know it might take three months before we'd get paid."

He was obviously upset about this turn of events. "If I had known this before, I'm not sure I would have been willing to participate. It's not because I don't believe in the mission, mind you, it's just that I didn't know how much we'd have to put up on the front end. I'll need to talk to the church council and my treasurer to see what we can do."

Rather than panic, Martha took stock of their situation and apologized to the Reverend for not communicating more clearly how long the payment process would take.

"Reverend, I'll talk to my staff and board president and see what we can do about the billing situation. I'm certain we can work this out without asking to you to take too big a risk." Although the Reverend was visibly concerned, he nodded his head in agreement and waited to hear the rest of the procedures.

Martha asked Evy to calculate the expected amount needed to operate the childcare portion of the program for up to three months. She then requested that Rev. Anderson go over the numbers separately with Evy so he would have a good idea of the amount his church might be expected to put up in advance each month. She then promised him that she would clarify the issue as soon as she looked over the numbers and spoke with Carlos, her board president.

"Of course, Martha," he replied. "I just want to be honest with you. I know how important the childcare is for the program, but if we don't have the money, it's better to know about it now."

Martha agreed. She knew that the childcare piece was absolutely critical for the other parts of the program to work and wanted to take care of Rev. Anderson's concerns immediately. In some ways, she felt she was already on shaky ground and the program was just starting! She thanked everyone for participating and let the group know that she was expecting the lead evaluator from the university that afternoon. No rest for the weary today.

After the meeting adjourned, Evy stayed to speak with Martha.

"I'm sorry about the situation with Reverend Anderson, Martha," Evy began. "I was just trying to lay out the basics of the reimbursement process."

"It's not your fault, Evy, you did a great job," Martha quickly replied.

"Well, that's the other thing I want to talk to you about," said Evy in a matter-of-fact way. "The job. I mean, I know you put money in the budget for me to do the accounting, but the reporting requirements on this contract are more involved than anything I've done in the past. And after Reverend Anderson's response, I would hate to be the reason that reimbursement was delayed."

Martha listened intently to what Evy was saying, but didn't speak.

"And honestly?" she added. "It would probably be less expensive to have someone do this part-time than pay me on an hourly basis."

Martha could see that Evy had a point and that she seemed to be taking a strong stand on the issue.

"Would you still be willing to be the tech consult?" she asked.

"Oh, of course!" said Evy, with an air of relief. She was glad that Martha was open to her suggestion and wasn't going to badger her to do the job.

Thirty minutes later, Julia brought two pieces of chocolate cake, Martha's favorite comfort food, to her office.

"That was a heck of a meeting!" Julia proclaimed, putting a piece of the cake in front of Martha and taking a bite of her own. "Talk about a roller coaster ride!"

Julia always seemed to know what Martha needed. Martha thanked her and reflected on the meeting as she pressed her fork into the cake. "I know what went wrong," she said as she began eating, "I wasn't prepared. I should have made it clear to Reverend Anderson that it could take a while to get reimbursed. I've put him in an uncomfortable position—he has to find funds or back out—which leaves us holding the bag for childcare."

Julia came to her defense. "Martha, we didn't have much time to put that proposal together. You had to take care of a thousand details. It's just one of those things."

Martha appreciated Julia's efforts but knew she had no time to indulge in self-blame. She savored a few more bites of cake as she pulled up the address book in her computer and found the number to Carlos' restaurant.

"Hi, Carlos. It's Martha from Helping Hands. We had our first meeting with our partners for the welfare-to-work grant today, and we've hit a few snags."

Over the din of the dwindling lunch crowd, Carlos listened to Martha describe the situation. "I had prepared *us* for how the state operates. What I hadn't done is tell Reverend Anderson that they would have to do pretty much the same thing," Martha lamented.

"Do you think we might lose him as a partner?" Carlos asked. "Would we have to take this on ourselves?"

"Well, we've committed to the state to include childcare, and it is in the budget, so funding isn't an issue. It's the administration and overhead that we're not in a position to cover. We're not a licensed childcare provider, and that application process is a nightmare. It would put us months behind in our CNA prep classes. Plus, we simply don't have space for a childcare program in our building. Another option would be to locate another partner from the community, but that would also be time consuming."

"Marta, if we have to find another partner, we'll do it," said Carlos. His relaxed and calm demeanor was reassuring.

Martha told him that Rev. Anderson had promised to get back to her once he talked with his council, so they decided not to panic until they heard more about the church's plans. Martha thanked Carlos for the support and said she'd keep him posted.

Julia popped her head back in Martha's office. "When it rains it pours, Martha. The evaluator from the university is waiting for you in the lobby."

With all the tumult from the morning meeting, Martha had lost track of time. She composed herself and went to greet the evaluator, with whom she had spoken briefly on the phone earlier in the week. She did not know what to expect, but was surprised to find a rather young looking woman sitting calmly in the lobby while several children played around her.

"Hello, I'm Martha White, you must be Professor Barr!" Martha said while trying to control her surprise at the relative youth of the faculty member who would be leading the evaluation of the welfare-to-work programs state-wide. "Welcome to Helping Hands!"

"Thank you," replied Dr. Barr with a warm smile, "but Annabelle, or just Belle, will do."

"That works for me, Belle. We're all pretty informal around here anyway," Martha replied as she began walking toward the offices.

Martha introduced Belle to her staff and gave her a brief tour of the facilities, pointing out where the CNA prep courses would be taught and the small computer room where clients could access computers loaded with self-paced GED prep software. Along the way, she learned that Dr. Barr had just finished her doctorate and had moved from Minnesota to join the faculty as an assistant professor in the School of Social Work at Martha's alma mater. It was her first semester of teaching.

"Have you had a chance to get to know Dr. Gault?" Martha asked as she was concluding the tour.

"I have," replied Dr. Barr. "As a matter of fact, he's the one who recommended me for this job."

"Really?" said Martha, still trying to get comfortable with the idea that this young woman, who didn't look much older than Linda, was a colleague of Dr. Gault.

"The School of Social Work has a research unit called the Center for Social Service Research. The Workforce Board extended the evaluation contract to the CSSR, and Dr. Gault recommended me for the lead research role. He said it would be a great way to get to know the state and develop data from which to publish. He also encouraged me to go around and meet all the project directors, and that's why I'm here today."

"Have you conducted evaluation research before?" Martha asked politely.

"As a doctoral student I was a research assistant for three years on a longitudinal evaluation project of programs that provided services to teen mothers," Dr. Barr replied, "and my dissertation is a comparative analysis of the levels of material hardship between those who married and those who remained single."

Martha felt a gradual sense of relief as it became clear that Belle was a serious researcher. She also knew that good marks from a university research evaluation could be beneficial to Helping Hands as it applied for other sources of funding. She was pleased that Dr. Barr's previous research was in the area of poverty, especially for young women. She asked about a research plan and was told that the contract required one site visit each year and that a report was due at the end of each fiscal year. Finally, Dr. Barr indicated that each program participant would be required to complete a brief "baseline" survey and that follow-up phone surveys would be conducted with clients after they had received services. The evaluation plan seemed straightforward and Martha foresaw no problems complying with this component of the welfare-to-work contract. She was also pleased to find out that Dr. Barr had set aside funds to remunerate survey participants for their responses.

Before saying her goodbyes, Martha took the opportunity to ask Dr. Barr for her input.

"Do you have any tips to share to make this new program a success?" Martha asked.

Dr. Barr thought for a moment. "Well, I think it's excellent that you have identified an employment niche, rather than just training per se," she began. "I guess the general advice I would offer is to make sure you really think through how you're going to market the program, and that you don't rely on a single referral source. Many of the the programs I studied in Minnesota didn't make their service goals because, for whatever reason, they just didn't get enough referrals."

The point hit home with Martha, and as she walked Dr. Barr to the exit, she made a mental note to speak with David, Linda, and Ruth about the different ways they could get the word out about the CNA prep course.

After the visit, Martha spent some time going through her e-mail. The new contract was consuming a great deal of time, but Helping Hands had other commitments to fulfill. There was an upcoming AIDS Walk fundraiser, and Martha was helping to organize a series of ongoing conference calls concerning the reauthorization of the welfare reform act. As she finished responding to e-mails, her phone rang, and as she reached to answer it, she was surprised to see that it was already 4:45.

"Martha, how are you?" Rev. Anderson asked. The lilt in the reverend's voice belied the tension and angst he had demonstrated at the meeting that morning. "I have some good news for you. I've shared the situation with the treasurer. He seems to think we can work it out. We may even do a special collection from the congregation just for this purpose."

"I can't tell you how happy this makes me, Reverend!" Martha said with relief.

"Well, haven't you heard, Martha? Since I'm going to a press conference with the governor, I'm a celebrity!" he joked. "They can't let me down!"

Martha laughed at his remark but still felt bad. "When you left this morning, I felt just awful. I apologize again for not communicating the billing procedures as clearly as I should have," Martha said humbly.

"It's okay, Martha," Rev. Anderson responded with a laugh. "Besides, what kind of church would we be if we didn't go the extra mile to help our community? I told you before that this whole town is my flock, and I like to think I back that up with action," he declared. "I'll let you know what we decide, but as for now, consider us on board."

When Martha hung up, she heaved a mental sigh of relief. She didn't even want to contemplate how they would have made things work without the afterhours childcare that Rev. Anderson was going to provide. She reflected on the ups and downs she had already experienced with the welfare-to-work project, and wondered if the program would even out or if she was going to be putting out fires for the next two years.

DECEMBER 2004

Martha pulled her car into the Helping Hands parking lot at seven a.m. She listened to the disk jockey give a weather report before turning off her radio.

"Good morning, River City!" blared the voice. "It's thirty-three degrees and there are some icy road conditions out there, so be careful driving into work this morning!"

Martha turned off the ignition and pulled her coat snugly against her before leaving the car. She arrived early this morning in expectation of another busy day. Requests for assistance always increased during the holidays, and Helping Hands was involved in other activities, such as its traditional Giving Tree assistance effort, which matched needy families with individuals willing to purchase gifts for them. The increase in requests for assistance was also due to marketing efforts that had been made to advertise the welfare-to-work program. Martha had passed out flyers at the CCS meeting in November, and Linda set up public service announcements, which had run on the radio for a month. Yet all the requests came from individuals seeking assistance with rent and utilities, with a smattering of requests for transportation assistance and work-related clothing.

By midday the PEACE ON EARTH banner that hung over the reception desk belied the frustration of the clients waiting to meet with a caseworker and the noise of the small children who crowded the lobby. David hurried into the break room and grabbed the now-empty coffee pot.

"Damn!" He swung open the refrigerator door and looked for a soda, desperate for some caffeine or sugar.

"David, your client is getting upset, you'd better go see what's up," Linda jokingly chided him on her way down the hall to the bathroom. David took a few deep breaths, shut the refrigerator door, and went back to his small office to interview a frustrated client. Word of mouth about the rent and utility assistance available had spread like wildfire. Helping Hands was able to offer larger amounts of assistance to people who qualified for the welfare-to-work program, but it was hard explaining the programmatic differences—and the smaller amounts of assistance—to those who did not qualify or could not provide sufficient documentation to satisfy the strict eligibility requirements that the Workforce Board had set in place. David's client could not understand why he was only eligible for a $50 voucher when his neighbor had received much more. It was a tough situation.

"Good morning, Helping Hands, this is Julia, how may I help you?" The phones had not stopped ringing all morning. "Yes, ma'am, we do provide rental assistance to qualified individuals. She listened for a minute and then responded. "I'm sorry, but as a landlord, you cannot apply for this assistance; your tenant would have to do that for herself." Julia's patience with the caller was wearing thin. "Yes, I understand you need the rent to be paid. Feel free to share our contact information with your tenant. However, he or she will need to make an appointment."

A few enterprising landlords had become aware of the rental assistance and now took it upon themselves to ask for the assistance directly.

No one at Helping Hands enjoyed disappointing clients, or worse, telling a client requesting rental assistance that all they could provide was a bag of groceries from the pantry. It was disheartening and becoming time-consuming to discriminate the eligibility criteria between programs. Stan, the semiretired, part-time accountant that Martha had hired to replace Evy, poked his head into Martha's office. Although dealing directly with clients was not his area of expertise, he had pitched in to help the staff through a very busy morning.

"Quite a party out there!" he half-way joked.

"I should have known that the word would get out quickly about the financial assistance," Martha replied, "but I'm a little worried that we're spending too much time on the emergency services and not enough on the CNA program.

"That's what I wanted to talk to you about," said Stan. "We're almost out of the funds we had dedicated to financial assistance for this quarter, and we haven't spent any of the funds we've set aside for the CNA program. Should I rob Peter to pay Paul?"

"Let's wait for the second quarter before we shift any funds," Martha replied with more than a hint of apprehension.

"Sure, I understand," Stan quickly replied. "But at this rate, we're going to run out of dedicated rental assistance funds by the end of the week—and right before the holidays, no less."

Martha mentally winced as she pictured families being evicted from their homes right before Christmas. "Let me review the terms of the grant again before we make a final decision, Stan. I'm pretty sure we can move a minimal amount of funds around in the budget without having to get approval from the Workforce Board first. Since the CNA courses are taking longer to get off the ground than expected, maybe this is a temporary adjustment we need to make."

"I know, it's a tough call," Stan sighed supportively. "But no matter what you decide, we're going to need to plan out the distribution of the rental assistance better. If we don't, we'll either blow through that part of our budget halfway through the grant, or run out of funds two weeks into every month."

"Point well taken," Martha replied, a bit frustrated. "Let me take a look at the grant and I'll get back to you before the end of the day."

Down the hall, Ruth took an application from Linda's desk and walked into the waiting room.

"Mrs. Deena Perkins?" She looked up and watched as a Caucasian woman in her late 40s got up and looked at her expectantly. She was dressed in black pants and a heavy jacket, and clutched her purse in front of her.

"I'm Deena. I heard about these new programs you offer from Carol Simpson at RCCC, and I thought I should come see if you can help me and my family," she said.

Ruth invited Deena into her office and looked over the application form Deena had filled out. Mrs. Perkins was a widow, whose husband Tom had passed away six years previously from a massive heart attack. She had two grown children and was caring for her two young grandchildren while holding down a job as a cashier at a convenience store. Deena had indicated that she was particularly interested in the CNA prep course, and Ruth was happy to have her first interested client.

Deena clearly felt uncomfortable with the notion of asking for help. "After my husband died, I received Survivor's Benefits for about two years, but even then I worked," she began. "I've never asked for a handout. If it weren't for my grandbabies, I wouldn't be here now."

It was clear to Ruth that Deena was under a great deal of stress.

"I applied to the community college for the certified nursing assistant program," Deena continued, "but when I talked to Carol, she suggested I contact you about a class you offer for folks who want to become CNAs. She also said you could provide childcare."

"That's right, Deena. I'll be happy to tell you all about our program and how it works. But you mentioned that you are taking care of your grandkids . . ."

"Well, two of them," Deena quickly replied.

"I'm a grandma too," Ruth noted, gesturing to a picture of herself with an adorable child of about two. "How long have you been taking care of them?"

"I've had Tina and Tommie for the past two years. I probably should tell you about their momma, but let me start with Joe, my oldest. I have two grown kids, Joe and Jackie. Joe never gave me no problems, and he was quite the man after his daddy passed. He did his best to look out for me and his sister. He lives in Dallas now and works for the cable company." Deena spoke quickly and in a no-nonsense fashion, and it was clear that she was quite proud of her son. "Now, that Jackie's another story altogether."

Deena explained how her daughter's life had spun out of control after her dad died, first with alcohol and drug use and then with turbulent relationships with multiple young men. Those relationships resulted in Jackie having two children, one at age sixteen and the other at eighteen. Eventually, Jackie and one of her boyfriends were arrested for selling drugs. Her previous legal problems as a juvenile collided with the state's mandatory sentencing laws, and as a result, Jackie was serving a three-year prison term.

Ruth asked about her current financial and household circumstances.

"I work part-time at a Stop 'n' Save market near my house, but I just don't make enough to pay for the things that the kids need," Deena explained. "I have a little bit of savings left from my husband's life insurance, but I don't have any health insurance, so I have to pay for everything on my own, and little Tommie has asthma." Deena paused after recounting these difficulties, and her eyes began to well with tears. She took a deep breath and continued. "I moved to River City so I could take care of Tommie and Tina and be closer to the prison so we can visit Jackie as much as possible, but it's still a tank of gas there and back and that ain't cheap."

Ruth nodded her head and affirmed that Deena was indeed facing some tough circumstances. She then asked for more information about her job.

"I like my boss," Deena quickly noted, "and he never puts me on the night shift because of the kids, but I can't do this much longer. I need to make more money and I'd rather work someplace where I could take care of people. It's what I've been doin' for as long as I can remember. Might as well get paid for it."

The list of financial challenges that Deena faced was considerable; Ruth needed to be as thorough and clear as possible. "Well, Deena," she began, "I think there are a number of ways we can help you." Deena's spirits improved when Ruth told her about the prep course, the childcare, and the emergency financial assistance available through the welfare-to-work program. Ruth also told her that she might be eligible for assistance from the Department of Child and Family Services. She knew that the state had begun to provide resources for kinship care providers, and was fairly certain that Deena would be eligible to receive assistance. Finally, while discussing Deena's monthly expenses, Ruth brought up the possibility of receiving a monthly earned income tax credit, and was surprised to learn that Deena had never heard of the EITC. To Deena a "tax rebate for working" sounded too good to be true, but Ruth explained that the program had been around for almost thirty years and had been significantly expanded during the Clinton administration. Because of her low wages and legal guardianship of her grandchildren, Deena would probably be eligible to receive several thousand dollars.

By the time Deena left Ruth's office she had been approved for the course and put on the list for Rev. Anderson's childcare. Ruth was especially pleased that she might be able to connect Deena with additional financial help. "If the other prep course students are like Deena," Ruth thought to herself, "I'm really going to enjoy teaching this class!"

In the office across the hall, Linda was interviewing a young Hispanic woman, Consuelo Hernandez, who, at nineteen, was seven months pregnant with her first child and recently separated from her husband. Consuelo had learned of the CNA prep course from a social worker at the domestic violence shelter where she spent six weeks recovering from the latest violent attack from her husband. She had left him, a veteran who had served in the early campaign of Operation Enduring Freedom in Afghanistan, after he lost his temper and beat her severely. Thanks to the efforts of the staff at the shelter, Consuelo had just moved into an apartment at the complex adjacent to the shelter property.

"How do you like your new place?" Linda asked. "She had referred several clients to the shelter and knew that the partnership the shelter had with the apartment complex was vital to the continued emotional and financial security of the clients it served. Linda had interned at a domestic violence shelter in Louisiana while completing her MSW and, shortly after moving to River City, had learned about the unique arrangement the shelter had managed to create with a large apartment complex that had been built next door. The project developers and owners of the buildings agreed to provide twenty apartments and lease them for three to twelve months as temporary housing for women leaving abusive relationships. Linda hoped Consuelo felt safe and secure and was glad that Helping Hands could help ease her transition to motherhood.

"It was very hard to leave Ricky," Consuelo told her. "Marriage and family is everything with my parents, and in their eyes, my leaving was a failure for me and for them. I didn't want them to be ashamed of me for not making my family work, but when Ricky lost it this last time, I worried I might lose my baby." Consuelo put her hands protectively on her stomach. "My family offered to let me stay with them, and I almost did that. But they can't help themselves; they would push me to go back to Ricky, and they would let him come around too so he could try to make up with me. I just had to do this," she finished with a note of resignation.

"You're very brave, Consuelo. Not only for taking the steps to protect yourself, but also for finding a way to support yourself financially," Linda replied. She moved the conversation to the subject of the CNA program and the prep course. "I think the program you've chosen at RCCC may be just the thing to get you started toward that goal. I see here that you earned your GED, and this will be your first time in a higher education setting."

"Yes, I always did okay in school, so I hope it won't be too hard," Consuelo said cheerfully. "I'd really like to be a registered nurse someday. I thought about it in high school, but I met Ricky and well, you know the rest."

Linda couldn't help but admire Consuelo's optimism. Though she faced daunting obstacles in extricating herself from an abusive marriage and preparing for motherhood and employment, Consuelo maintained an undeniable level of confidence in her own future. Linda explained how the prep course would be structured, and that participants would have childcare provided by Rev. Anderson's evening program. Consuelo was particularly excited to learn that if she passed both the prep course and the CNA program, she would earn assistance with her childcare costs once employed.

"The good news," said Linda, "is that you are on the list for the first class!" She hesitated, and then regretfully added, "unfortunately, it doesn't look like we're going to offer the prep course any time soon. As far as I know, you're the only person who has signed up, and Ruth wants at least half a dozen people in each course."

Consuelo looked crestfallen. She had naïvely hoped to be able to finish both programs before her baby was born, but now she wasn't even sure if she would have the opportunity to finish the prep course before the baby was due.

"I'm really sorry, Consuelo," Linda consoled, "but I promise we will do everything we can to help you through both courses when the time comes. Okay?"

A slight smile returned to Consuelo's face. "My *abuela* says that everything happens for a reason. I haven't quite figured that one out yet," she said half-heartedly, "but I'll be ready when you are."

"Good! That's the spirit!" Linda replied encouragingly. "Now let's go find Ruth. I think you're going to like her." Linda found Ruth in the copy room and made the introduction, then walked with Consuelo to the bus stop before heading back into the office.

As the workday neared its end, Linda and Ruth shared with Martha their excitement over Deena and Consuelo, the first two prospects they'd had for the CNA prep course. The critical component of the program they had laboriously put together was finally getting off the ground. Ruth asked Martha if she was right to suggest to Deena that she was entitled to some financial assistance for the care of her grandchildren.

"Absolutely!" exclaimed Martha. "The state has finally gotten on the bandwagon and accessed federal funds for kinship care. Grandparents and other relatives have been stepping up to the plate for years, with no help at all from the state. It's about time they get some financial assistance, just like other foster care providers."

"And the kids would be eligible for health insurance under CHIP, wouldn't they?" added Linda.

"Yes," Martha confirmed. "Deena could also pursue different custodial arrangements, such as subsidized permanent guardianship, that give the caregiver some legal rights over the children but don't require that parental rights be terminated."

Martha said that it had been a few years since she had worked in child welfare, but she did know that families often avoided the formal child welfare system because in the past it had forced parental rights to be terminated and often turned family members against each other. "Now," she continued, "the system gives families options they feel better about and also gives them some well-deserved financial support."

Hearing this made Ruth very happy. "What's the name of the supervisor you know at the Department of Child and Family Services?" she asked Martha.

"Rebecca Thomas," Martha responded. "Call her and find out what you can for Mrs. Perkins. And make sure to tell Becky I said hello!"

Switching subjects, Ruth thanked Linda for introducing her to Consuelo. "What a sweetheart," Ruth added.

"I do worry about her though," Linda said. "She has an abusive soon-to-be ex-husband, and it doesn't sound as though he has accepted her leaving him. It might get tougher for her after the baby is born, especially if she keeps feeling pressured by her family to get back together with him." Linda paused before continuing. "She reminds me of a client I worked with during my internship. Two days after she left the shelter and moved into her new place, her ex found her and shot her to death. Then he grabbed the kids and led the police on a chase. It was all over the news in New Orleans."

The room went silent.

"Well anyway, what reminds me about her is Consuelo's enthusiasm for life and her excitement about making it on her own." Linda suddenly lowered her voice. "I don't know what I'd do if something like that happened again," she mumbled.

Martha reassured Linda and softly patted her on the back. "We'll do the best we can to help her, and remember, she knows how to access resources, not only with us but with the shelter folks too."

AUGUST 2005

Martha could not believe that the program had been up and running for almost a year. In June, Dr. Barr had made a site visit to evaluate the program. Despite the initial hesitation Martha had felt due to her youth, Dr. Barr had proven herself to be a thorough and competent researcher. She told Martha that the evaluation report would consist of three main parts: a description of Helping Hands and issues related to the performance of the welfare-to-work program, a statistical breakdown of demographic information gleaned from the baseline surveys that each eligible welfare-to-work participant filled out, and finally, information from a follow-up telephone survey that Dr. Barr was in the process of conducting with individuals who had received services in the first six months of the program. Dr. Barr asked wide-ranging questions about Helping Hands: its history, mission, operating budget, and personnel, among other things, and Martha walked her through the process a typical client in the welfare-to-work program would experience, from the initial intake interview with one of the caseworkers to the childcare vouchers that were offered to graduates of the CNA program. Dr. Barr spoke to each staff member involved in the program, and at the end of the day, Martha took her to meet Rev. Anderson, who proudly gave her a tour of his facilities and, true to form, interspersed his interview with funny anecdotes about the children. Finally, Dr. Barr sat through one of Ruth's prep courses and stayed afterwards to speak to several of the students. It was a long and exhausting day, but Martha was satisfied that Dr. Barr had been given a very realistic portrait of what happened on a day-to-day basis.

The one issue that Martha had been worried about—the lower-than-expected number of individuals who had enrolled in the CNA prep course—turned out to be a nonissue. Dr. Barr told Martha that many of the programs she had visited across the state also had problems meeting early performance goals, and that it was clear that the numbers enrolling in the prep course had improved after the first few months. Martha was glad to see that Dr. Barr had noticed, because the increase in numbers had come from efforts she, Ruth, and Linda had made to contact every residential nursing care facility in River City. In addition, Ruth had worked out a plan with Carol to contact every new registrant for the CNA course at the community college. After speaking with Ruth, many of those who had registered for the course decided that the assistance that Helping Hands offered was worth the extra time it would take to complete the prep course.

It was lunchtime and Martha was on the phone with her daughter, Jessie, who had just started her junior year of high school, when she heard David yell from the lunchroom. After telling Jessie she would call her back, Martha hung up the phone and decided to see what all the commotion was about. Walking down the hall, she could tell that most of the staff had already gathered in the break room. She entered the room and could see David fidgeting with the rabbit ears on the small television that sat on the counter.

"That hurricane going through the Gulf?" David said as he made some final adjustments, "It's hitting New Orleans." David stepped away as the picture cleared and a local weatherman pointed to the massive storm that occupied almost the entire gulf region.

"This is not a category five storm anymore," said the weatherman with hesitant optimism, "but it's going to do some serious damage to New Orleans and other parts of the Mississippi Gulf."

Martha looked at Linda and watched as the color drained from her face.

Questions for Discussion

1. In the beginning of the chapter, the welfare-to-work program put together by Helping Hands gets off to a flashy start as Rev. Anderson and other faith-based leaders get invited to a press conference with the governor. Do you think prominent politicians should emphasize the participation of faith-based organizations in the delivery of government-funded services? Do you think working in a faith-based social service organization would be different from working in a secular service agency? In what ways?

2. In the chapter, Martha meets Dr. Barr, the lead evaluator of the welfare-to-work grant, and learns about the different components of the evaluation. One component that Dr. Barr mentions is a brief baseline survey that all new program participants will be required to complete. What types of information would you include in a baseline survey of the Helping Hands welfare-to-work program? How would this information be helpful?

3. Program evaluations can take many forms, but in general, evaluations consider the process (or implementation) of the program and outcomes related to program activity. What is the value of an external evaluation of program implementation and outcomes? To funding agencies? To contract agencies? To researchers?

4. Ruth's client, Deena Perkins, was surprised to learn that she was eligible to receive money through an Earned Income Tax Credit (EITC). Though the EITC typically receives less attention than Temporary Assistance for Needy Families (TANF), the federal government spends much more money on the program (over $40 billion in 2008). Why would the EITC, which offers tax credits to low-income working families, be popular with both conservatives and liberals?

5. A major component of the welfare-to-work program set up by Helping Hands is an educational training program designed to improve the success rates of individuals studying to become Certified Nursing Assistants. Are you aware of any government subsidized job training programs in your community? If so, what types of job training are offered?

6. Helping Hands had initial problems finding enough eligible participants for its CNA prep course. Indeed, recruitment and outreach is often an overlooked component to an effective social service program. Enumerate the ways in which the staff at Helping Hands tried to recruit participants. What other methods could have been used? What if the welfare-to-work program had taken place in a rural area? What marketing techniques could be used in a sparsely populated area with no local television, newspaper, or radio?

Innovative Assignments

1. Explore kinship care and related permanency options offered to family caregivers. What programs does the federal government support and fund?

What options does your state offer? How active is your state in promoting these services to family caregivers? Provide data on the number of families accessing these services.

2. Research various states' approaches to the administration of economic assistance and child welfare services. Interview high level officials in these states to ascertain not only why the state chose to structure services in this way, but how well this structure ultimately serves clients, from the perspective of the administration. Contact information for commissioners and their deputies is typically found on each state's official government Web site.

3. Within the first quarter of operating the grant program, Martha is faced with the decision to move funds from one part of the program to another, even though she clearly planned to focus on the CNA program as a signature piece. This means she had money in her childcare budget that could be used to help individuals in other ways but would move funds away from the CNA program that she might want to use later that year. Talk to at least three agency directors whose agencies operate on grant funds about similar situations they have faced. What factors do they use to decide when and how best to shift funds during a budget year? Are they required to ask permission from the funding source before doing so? On what areas did they expect to spend significant funds but found their assumptions to be wrong?

Suggested Readings

Beverly, S. (2002). What social workers need to know about the earned income tax credit. *Social Work*, 47(3), 259–266.

Braman, D., & Wood, J. (2003). From one generation to the next: How criminal sanctions are reshaping family life in urban America. In J.Travis & M. Waul, (Eds.), *Prisoners once removed: The impact of incarceration and reentry on children, families, and communities.* Washington DC: Urban Institute Press.

Braverman, M. T., Constantine, N. A., & Slater, J. K. (2004). *Foundations and evaluation: Contexts and practices for effective philanthropy.* San Francisco: Jossey-Bass.

Christopher, K. (2005). The poverty line forty years later: Alternative poverty measures and women's lives. *Race, Gender & Class*, 12(2), 34–53.

Edin, K., Kefalas, M., & Reed, J. (2004, November). A peek inside the black box: What marriage means for poor unmarried parents. *Journal of Marriage and the Family*, 1007–1014.

Gray, A. (2003). *Collaboration in public services: The challenge for evaluation.* New Brunswick, NJ: Transaction.

Kennedy, S., & Bielefeld, W. (2002). Government shekels without government shackles? The administrative challenges of charitable choice. *Public Administration Review*, 62(1), 4–11.

Kennedy, S., & Bielefeld, W. (2006). *Charitable choice at work: Evaluating faith-based job programs in the states.* Washington, DC: Georgetown University Press.

Kissane, R. J. (2007). How do faith-based organizations compare to secular providers? Nonprofit directors' and poor women's assessments of FBOs. *Journal of Poverty, 11*(4), 91–116

Milliken C. S., Auchterlonie, J. L., & Hoge, C. W. (2007). Longitudinal assessment of mental health problems among active and reserve component soldiers returning from the Iraq War. *JAMA, 298*(18), 2141–2148.

Morgan, K. (2001). A child of the sixties: The great society, the new right, and the politics of federal childcare. *Journal of Political History, 13*(2), 215–250.

National Coalition Against Domestic Violence. (n.d.). *Domestic Violence in the Military.* Available at http://www.ncadv.org

Radey, M. (2008). Frontline welfare work: Understanding social work's role. *Families in Society, 89*(2), 193–201.

Roberts-DeGennaro, M., & Fogel, S. L. (2007). Faith-based and community initiative: Service providers and approaches to studying service outcomes. *Journal of Policy Practice, 6*(2), 45–62.

CHAPTER 5

After the Storm

AUGUST 29, 2005

Martha fumbled with her keys as she stood outside the back door of Helping Hands in the late August heat. She locked the door and let out a sigh of exhaustion as she brushed the sweat beading on her forehead. She and the staff had stayed late, all eyes glued to the break room television as the story of Hurricane Katrina's landfall unfolded before their eyes. Martha could not remember ever having seen a storm as massive as Katrina—it filled the entire Gulf of Mexico! She and the staff—Linda in particular—sat waiting, silent in thought, many silently praying as the storm battered New Orleans and the Gulf Coast. Once it was clear that it would be hours before they knew the true outcome of the storm, they all huddled around Linda, ensuring her that everything would be okay. Linda had not been able to get any of her family on the phone. She left with Ruth, agreeing after much convincing to let Ruth stay with her the remainder of the evening as she tried to contact her family.

As she walked to her car, Martha was astounded at how silent and still the night was in River City. She could hear the crickets whirring and could even make out a few bright stars through the orange glow of the city lights as she gazed up at the late-summer sky. "How odd," she thought. "It's so calm and peaceful . . . and people in New Orleans are fighting for their lives at this very minute."

Martha was lost deep in thought as she drove across town on her way home from the office. Her thoughts wandered, passing from concern for Linda and her family in New Orleans to prayers for those in the path of the storm all across the Gulf Coast. She and her husband had been caught in a bad storm in the Caribbean on their honeymoon, and Martha would never forget how scared she felt huddled in her hotel room for two days, listening to the wind and the rain batter their windows. Arriving at home, Martha entered through the door from the garage, her daughter and husband yelling hello to her from the living room as she entered the kitchen.

"There's leftovers for you in the fridge, Mom," Martha's daughter, Jessie, shouted. Martha made a mental note to herself to limit the late hours spent at Helping Hands. Both she and Allen, her husband, had frequently been working late, and the twins were making dinner for themselves more often. Even though the circumstances at work had been unusual, she felt pangs of guilt for missing dinner again.

"Mom," Jessie yelled impatiently as she heard Martha take the leftovers out of the refrigerator. "What took you so long?"

"I'm sorry, sweetie," Martha began to explain as she walked into the family room with a bowl of cold macaroni and cheese. She walked over to her husband, who was sitting on the couch, paging through the newspaper. She leaned over, gave him a kiss, then plopped down next to Jessie, giving her daughter a big peck on the cheek. "I got stuck at the office with my staff. Believe it or not, we were glued to the television watching footage of Hurricane Katrina."

Brandon, her strapping sixteen-year-old son, walked through the room on his way to the kitchen. "Hey Mom," he said casually.

"Did you make this, Brandon? Because this is some good mac 'n' cheese," Martha said as she ate a few more spoonfuls.

"It's the only thing he *can* make," Jessie quickly added. "Good thing it comes in a box with directions!"

Brandon shot his sister a look but said nothing as he poured himself some sweet tea from a pitcher in the refrigerator. He walked back from the kitchen and headed upstairs to his bedroom.

Brandon was not known for taking a crack from his sister without responding, so Martha glanced at her husband and Jessie quizzically.

"He's upset about his coach," Jessie jumped in immediately.

"His coach?" Martha asked, still not understanding.

"Seems that Coach Johnson is stuck in New Orleans," Allen said as he peered over the top of the paper. "Went for a coaching conference and couldn't get a flight out before they closed the airport."

"That explained Brandon's mood," Martha thought to herself. Her son idolized his coach.

"One of my friends at school, you know Seana, right?" Jessie continued. "Well, her grandma lives in Mississippi near the beach. They don't know if she left in time or if she is still there."

"I'm sorry about your friend's grandmother, honey," Martha answered. "But that's why I was late tonight. Linda, one of my caseworkers, couldn't get in touch with her family either."

With his nose still in the paper, Allen switched channels and found a national station that was covering the storm. The nightly news anchor came on live, standing in the surprisingly dry streets of the New Orleans central business district.

"This is amazing news to report from New Orleans tonight," the reporter proclaimed, a sense of relief exuding from his words and gestures. "America, I am happy to report that it appears New Orleans has dodged the worst of Hurricane Katrina. While we are receiving reports of wind and water damage, it seems the Big Easy has waged the war against Katrina and won, with the eye of the storm hitting just east of the metropolitan New Orleans area."

"Did you hear that?" Jessie exclaimed. "That is so awesome! Can you believe it?" She jumped off the couch and ran upstairs to tell Brandon.

Martha could hardly believe what she had heard. New Orleans had weathered the storm. She didn't have the heart to point out to her daughter, at least not tonight, that if the storm made landfall east of New Orleans then it most likely made a direct hit on the Mississippi coast, where Seana's grandmother resided. "They're not reporting anything on Mississippi for some reason tonight," she justified to herself. "Hopefully that means the news is as good there as in New Orleans."

That night, as Martha crawled under the covers, she said a simple prayer of thanks, and hoped that Linda and Jessie's friend would hear good news from their families the following day.

Martha rolled over in bed early the next morning, woken by the sound of Allen getting ready for work. As she waited for Allen to get out of the shower, she decided to turn the television on to catch a bit of the morning news. What she saw and heard made her instantly sit upright in bed.

The same news anchor from the night before was standing in the same spot in the central business district of New Orleans as he was less than twelve hours earlier, but this time, water was rising around him, already up to his mid-calves. "Something is terribly wrong in New Orleans," he proclaimed. "Where we thought New Orleans escaped the worst yesterday, it now seems that the levees that keep this city dry—a city which sits below sea level—must have been breeched in some way. We do not yet have any confirmed reports of what exactly has gone wrong, but as you can see, the water is gradually rising around me on streets that were dry just hours ago." The reporter seemed stunned, not even sure what to say next.

Martha felt a big lump rise in her throat, and a temporary wave of panic rushed through her. Growing up in River City, she had experienced enough floods to know that sometimes the worst part came after the rains. "Oh my God," she thought to herself. "It's not over yet."

Martha sat glued to the television for another forty-five minutes before she was able to peel herself away to hurriedly get ready for work. By the time she reached the office, she was late. As she walked through the back door at Helping Hands, Martha encountered a scene similar to the evening before. David, Julia, and a few volunteers from the food pantry were gathered around the television in the break room, completely silent, barely turning their heads to acknowledge Martha's arrival.

Martha stepped into the break room, standing quietly behind the staff sitting at the table. She could hardly believe what was unfolding before her eyes on the television. It was noticeably worse than what she had seen earlier in the morning. Aerial shots of various levee breeches in New Orleans were running across the screen. Entire neighborhoods of the city were filling up with water. People were coming out of their homes, some on rafts, some in boats, some wading or swimming, all fleeing the rising water. "This is an American tragedy unfolding before our eyes," she heard the reporter lament.

After watching more coverage, Martha reluctantly pulled herself and the staff away from the television, promising them that they could leave the news on all day to check updated reports between clients. She found it hard to leave those images, but knew they had to keep things going at Helping Hands all the same. Checking her messages, she found a voicemail from Ruth.

"Martha, this is Ruth." Ruth's voice sounded tired and strained. "I'm at Linda's house. I stayed here all night. She got through to her parents last night, but her parents haven't been able to find out anything about her grandmother, who lives in a nursing facility. Linda is really worried about her grandmother. *Fíjate*, I'm pretty worried myself, so if you don't mind, I think I'll stay here with Linda. Call me on my cell phone if you need me. We're trying to keep Linda's home phone line open in case her family calls. *Hasta luego, Martha.*"

While Martha had a sense that this would be one of those days that she would really need Ruth at the office, it was comforting to know that Ruth was there to support Linda. Before she could even give Ruth a call back to let her know it was okay, David came running into her office.

"Martha, you have to come back to the break room now!" he said breathlessly.

Martha rushed down to the break room behind David, where the staff had congregated once again. This time, the little black and white television was filled with even more horrific images than before. News helicopters were filming residents of New Orleans literally chopping through their roofs with axes and climbing out of their attics to escape the rising flood waters. Wherever the news camera panned, there were women, children, men, elderly, infants, and pets clinging to life on top of their roofs. Surrounded by water, there was literally nowhere else to go. One family had spelled HELP with a collection of sneakers, hoping to attract rescue. Martha felt sick to her stomach.

"I can't believe what I'm seeing," Julia exclaimed, her eyes wide with horror. "How could this happen? How could all these people just be stuck there? I mean, this is America! Come on! Somebody do something!" She yelled at the television.

David turned up the volume on the television. The same news anchor was reporting the events as they transpired, looking weary and horrified himself. "The city of New Orleans has a public shelter at the Superdome on the edge of downtown. It appears as if people are attempting to wade, swim, and boat for miles to get to safety there."

The aerial camera panned over the Superdome, showing people gradually making their way through block after block, foot upon foot of brown, dirty water. Parents held babies above their heads, barely keeping their own heads above water. As the news helicopter turned back toward some of the neighbor-hoods leading away from the Superdome, it showed family upon family sitting on their roofs, waving in desperation for rescue. As far as the eye could see, New Orleans was underwater.

"Why doesn't this stupid news helicopter start picking people off the roofs and take them to the Superdome?" David proclaimed angrily. "How can they just fly around and look at everyone and not do anything about it?"

Martha was having a hard time coming to grips with what she was wit-nessing on the television. It didn't square with the response she remembered seeing on the news when Florida had been hit with multiple hurricanes the previous summer. "There have to be plans in the works to help these people!" is all she could summon to allay the disbelief and fear that she and her staff were feeling.

"Where's President Bush, the governor of Louisiana, the mayor of New Orleans, FEMA, the national guard . . . ?" Julia questioned out loud. "I mean, the city is below sea level, it sits in a hurricane zone . . . there's got to be an emergency plan!"

"We can send troops to the other side of the world to fight a war, but we can't rescue people in one of our own cities? This can't be happening!" David blurted out, still watching scenes of helicopters flying over what looked like a large lake with homes sticking out of it.

"Maybe FEMA and the federal government are waiting for the state gov-ernment to make an official request for help," Martha offered. "Or there's some kind of red tape impeding the process." Martha tried again to justify what was transpiring. She wasn't buying her own words at this point.

"Red tape my *you-know-what*," David jeered. "There are people dying in front of our eyes! It's time to get a little creative—no, a LOT creative!"

Martha could hear the phone ringing at the front desk. "As much as I wish we could stay in here and watch how this continues to unfold, we have to get some work done today. We've got clients waiting in the lobby and the phone is ringing nonstop," Martha stated, trying to convince herself as much as her staff that it was necessary to pull away from the news coverage. Watch-ing made her feel helpless, but also made her want to help. She suspected the staff felt the same.

Back in her office, Julia beeped in on the intercom. "Martha, you are not going to believe this, but we're getting calls from people in the community asking if they can drop off donations for the Katrina victims."

"Really?" said Martha, surprised at first by the news but encouraged that people in River City thought of Helping Hands as an organization that would be able to get help to people.

"Four calls in the last twenty minutes," Julia repeated. "What do you want me to tell them?"

"Well, I guess there is no reason for us not to accept the donations," Martha replied, thinking on her feet. "If nothing else, we could transfer it to the Red Cross. Tell them we'll accept nonperishable food donations and clothes and blankets. Is there room to store it in the food pantry?"

"Last I checked, we had space to squeeze it in," Julia stated.

Martha jumped in quickly, "Okay, then, let's start accepting donations. I'll get on the phone with CCS to see if other agencies are experiencing the same thing."

Martha called Thomas Jenkins, chair of the CCS. He told her that she was the third nonprofit executive director that had called him so far that morning. They agreed that it seemed appropriate to call an emergency meeting of the CCS.

Martha hung up the phone and began to gather her thoughts as David again appeared in her doorway. "Martha, you're not going to believe this, but my last two appointments just brought stuff in for the Katrina victims. Can you believe it?"

David and Martha were both humbled and inspired by the generosity demonstrated by his clients, individuals struggling just as much in their own way, but eager to reach out and help their neighbors in the face of disaster. Martha then sent an e-mail to Evy asking her to update the Helping Hands Web site as a place where Katrina donations would be accepted.

By the end of the day, Helping Hands' clients, people from the neighborhood, and agency supporters had brought bottled water, diapers, canned food, flashlights, clothes, and other material to help the victims of Hurricane Katrina. The Helping Hands staff stacked the donations into the food pantry and the clothes closet. The next morning, a pile of donations blocked the front door of the building. In a few days, the food pantry was not able to hold all the material that was being donated, so each night after work she, Allen, and the twins loaded the supplies into their truck and took them to the central headquarters of the Salvation Army.

Ruth returned to work, having stayed with Linda the day after the storm hit as she tried to contact her family and get word of her grandmother's whereabouts. Linda's parents had left at the last minute after receiving word that the mayor of New Orleans had issued a mandatory evacuation, but they had not been able to take Linda's grandmother, who was living in a nursing home when the storm hit. Ruth was visibly worn down by the activities of the past few days.

The CCS meeting had been scheduled for the end of the week. It was now clear that the recovery from Hurricane Katrina would take many months, and state and city governments in the path of Katrina, indeed, across the entire country, would need to organize their efforts to assist those whose homes and lives had met with a disaster of epic proportions.

"Ay, tengo sueño," Ruth yawned in the car. Martha took note of Ruth's unusual reticence and let her close her eyes and rest on the way to the meeting.

"We're lucky," Martha thought as she pulled into the parking lot, "that we don't have a prep course scheduled for this week." The schedule for the

CNA prep course was closely tied to the schedule of the CNA course that was offered at RCCC, and there was little room for deviation.

Martha and Ruth entered the United Way building and surveyed the room. The meeting was about to begin and was so crowded that people were standing in the back and along the walls. Martha noticed a small group of unfamiliar faces who looked like they might be city or state employees from the identification badges they wore clipped to their shirts. She also saw Rev. Anderson standing with a few other clergy members.

Thomas quickly began the meeting. "Hey everyone, thanks for coming. For those of you who don't know me, I'm Thomas Jenkins, chair of the CCS and Executive Director of the River City Children's Home." He surveyed the room, taking a mental role of all in attendance. "We're here to discuss how CCS can best organize a rapid response to the needs of Hurricane Katrina victims."

Thomas continued, turning to the new attendees. "First, however, I'd like to introduce the River City Emergency Operations Team. They have some breaking news to share, so I'm going to turn the floor over to them."

Thomas stepped out of the way, as one of the guests stood to speak.

"Greetings everyone. I'm LaShonda Harrison, Director of Emergency Operations for River City. As I am sure all of you are aware, the situation in New Orleans continues to rapidly deteriorate. We have all seen and heard on the news how the Superdome is at capacity and there are now thousands of people stranded at the New Orleans Convention Center. The word from city officials is that the shelter conditions at the Superdome are no longer safe, sanitary, or secure, and that they are now working with the state of Louisiana, FEMA, the National Guard, and other law enforcement agencies to evacuate as many people as possible. Basically, their goal is to have everyone out of the city by the end of the week as they now expect the flooding conditions to continue for three weeks or more. The word today is that eighty percent of New Orleans is underwater."

Martha surveyed the crowd quietly as LaShonda spoke. The expressions of shock, concern, and disbelief were evident from person to person.

LaShonda continued, "River City will serve as a host city for evacuees. The governor has just made it official. What this means is that in the next few days, perhaps even by tomorrow, busloads of evacuees will begin to arrive and will be housed at the convention center downtown. We are already making plans with the Red Cross and Salvation Army to assist in setting up the mass care shelter, but we will need help from the entire community to house a large number of evacuees."

The clergy member standing next to Rev. Anderson spoke up.

"Ms. Harrison, how many evacuees do you think will come to River City, and what sort of assistance do you need from us, both the nonprofit and faith community?"

There was a bit of hesitation in LaShonda's response. "At this point, it's just a guess, but it could be five thousand people or even more. We'll need volunteers around the clock to help intake the evacuees as they arrive. Many of them will arrive with no identification or possessions and we expect that some families will arrive separated from one another. We may even have some children who were separated from their parents during helicopter evacuations. So we'll need trained professionals to conduct intake interviews and to assist us in tracking down family members. We'll also need medical professionals on hand and plenty of volunteers to help cook and serve meals and coordinate donations."

"What about mental health needs?" asked the director of a local crisis counseling center. "Is the city planning on having counselors available to help the survivors deal with their trauma and grief?"

"We will certainly need qualified volunteers who can offer crisis counseling," LaShonda replied. "But our first priority is to meet the physical and safety needs of the evacuees and to reunify families."

The CCS members spent the rest of the morning working with LaShonda and her staff on a coordinated plan to assist with the shelter operations. Martha and Ruth committed time from their staff to assist with the intake interviews, something that was an area of expertise for Helping Hands, especially since the welfare-to-work grant started.

The staff spent the next two weeks working shifts at the convention center, serving countless evacuees. Every day at noon, Martha debriefed staff as they changed shifts at the shelter. She had noticed that the work was weighing on them and was concerned that they might suffer secondary trauma from their work with the survivors. It was impossible not to be affected by the stories of death, loss, and survival. As the staff shared their stories, Martha did her best to process their experiences with them. But at times, the sheer intensity of the hardships that evacuees had faced and the growing realization of the ways in which government ineptitude and, it seemed, indifference, had contributed to the problem, was almost too much to bear.

Martha sat behind her desk early on a Wednesday morning. She had been arriving early and staying late since Helping Hands had begun to participate in the outreach effort to evacuees, but the regular work of the agency also needed to be maintained. She reviewed, for a second time, the evaluation report that she had received from the Workforce Board. Dr. Barr had conducted her evaluation visit three months earlier and at that time, Martha was feeling good about their progress. Now she felt as overwhelmed as she did nearly a year ago when they began the welfare-to-work program. Martha took a drink of coffee and began outlining notes for her annual report to the board. Carlos had graciously reserved a private room at his restaurant for the next day's meeting and would also be handing the role of board president to Carlene for a two-year term. Martha reflected on how much had happened in the past year, from their early struggles with the CNA prep course enrollment and the emergency financial assistance budget to being thrust into the middle of disaster relief for the thousands of evacuees who had come to River City after the hurricane.

She sat lost in thought over all that had happened. "There is so much to tell, I'm not sure where to begin," she said to herself. The evaluation report contained many sources of data: monthly tallies of service productivity that Martha and her staff provided to the Workforce Board, as well as findings and observations Dr. Barr and her research team had put together from the site visit and from baseline and telephone surveys that had been completed by welfare-to-work clients. She wanted to provide the board with key points from Dr. Barr's evaluation, since she knew they would be particularly interested in the highlights of the report.

Martha smiled to herself as she reviewed one element of which she was particularly proud. After fearing the CNA prep course might not get off the ground, a year later, Ruth's class had been offered to forty-five people, and all but of four of them had graduated. This was in large part due to good case-work, Ruth's flexibility and willingness to offer make-up sessions during the day, and Rev. Anderson's childcare program. She had heard from a few clients that their children "just loved" the people taking care of them at the church, and apparently Rev. Anderson was a grandpa-like figure for the children. He would often show up to read to the children or organize a game of Go Fish, and even drove the church van from time to time. Ruth's reputation as a dynamo was only enhanced by the way she threw herself into the class, making changes to the schedule as best she could to accommodate students, but also holding them accountable for completing the requirements. Martha relished the chance to sing their praises to the board. Harkening back to the board meeting where she had first mentioned the welfare-to-work opportunity, Martha recalled Ron Tripp's initial caution about getting involved in the program. She smiled when she thought of showing him all the good they had done for people.

They had also managed to stay within the first year budget goal, moving funds around as needed to compensate for increased demand in one area or to cover extra daycare, which was often needed. The state funding agency allowed grantees the ability to make budget adjustments without prior approval, as long as they were not requesting additional funds. This fact made life much easier for project directors like Martha. Finally, though a bit of a grump, Stan was proving to be an valuable addition to the staff. He had retired from the state comptroller's office and was particularly adept at delineating the welfare-to-work budget from other, smaller grants that helped fund the day-to-day services that Helping Hands provided.

Though Martha was proud of the effort her staff had made to address previously unmet needs in River City, some of the findings from the six-month follow-up survey that Dr. Barr had conducted with welfare-to-work partici-pants were cause for concern. Though Dr. Barr found that over ninety percent of respondents indicated that the rent and utility assistance had helped them to avoid being evicted or having utilities shut off, she also found that within six months of receiving assistance, the majority of respondents continued to experience, as Dr. Barr put it, "housing-related hardships." Many respondents had at least one utility, such as a phone or electricity, shut off in the interim, and a small but significant number had been evicted or forced to move because of their inability to pay rent. As part of the welfare-to-work contract, Helping Hands offered up to $300 in a three-month period for rent or utility assistance. This was more than Helping Hands was able to offer through its other programs, but it was apparently not enough to prevent participants from continuing to experience housing instability. Martha knew the budget was tight, and any increase Helping Hands could offer in the way of rent or utility assistance would result in serving fewer people. It was the classic quantity vs. quality tradeoff that bedeviled social service agencies.

The other finding from the telephone survey that had not been anticipated was the way in which limited childcare availability in River City conflicted with the twelve-hour, weekend, and nightshift schedules that newly employed CNAs were often given. Qualitative comments that Dr. Barr collected from survey respondents indicated that many were not able to benefit from the childcare vouchers that Helping Hands offered because they worked shifts for which no formal childcare was available. She would take the primary findings from the evaluation to the Board and see what they had to say.

At eight a.m., Julia poked her head in Martha's door. "Hey boss, already been here a while, eh?"

"Guilty as charged," Martha said with a smile that did not entirely hide her fatigue.

"Thought you'd want to know that Linda left a message on my voice mail." Julia said as she handed Martha a note. "She left her cell number and wanted you to call her as soon as you could."

Martha took the number from Julia and, glancing at the early hour, decided to call Linda in an hour or two. Linda had taken a leave of absence and returned to Louisiana after the storm, which had taken a huge personal toll on her and her family. The marshy lands where her parents lived in a parish outside of New Orleans had been hit particularly hard. And though her parents and siblings had safely evacuated to Shreveport, Linda had learned just before she left River City that her grandmother had been too frail to leave the nursing home where she was placed. No one knew what had happened to the residents.

The last word Martha had heard was that Linda was with her family in Shreveport, and planned to go back home once the National Guard would allow people to return. Martha called Linda later that morning. She answered the phone on the first ring, but her voice cracked as she spoke.

"Martha, I have some terrible news," she began. "We found out that the nursing home didn't evacuate the residents before the hurricane. My grandma drowned when the building flooded."

"Oh my lord, Linda! I am so, so sorry!" Martha replied. She tried to maintain her composure but couldn't help herself. Her eyes filled with tears and she began to softly cry.

"We don't know all the details," Linda continued in a quivering voice, "but from what the owner told my parents, many of the residents were so medically fragile that they couldn't be moved in time. Why they waited so long . . ." She broke off and took a deep breath before continuing. "I know this will put you in an awful bind, Martha, but there is no way I can come back to work any time soon. We're still waiting for permission to go back and see what happened to my parents' house. I have to be with my parents through this, and I don't know what we'll find once we do get home. I hope you understand."

"You have to take care of you and your family before you can take care of anyone else, Linda. We'll manage things here. I don't want you worrying about us with all that you have to cope with right now. I can't begin to say how sorry I am," Martha answered.

"I'll do my best to get back to River City as soon as I can," said Linda, "but honestly? I don't know what's going to happen. I feel so helpless right now. I just want to scream at the people who left my grandmother to drown." Linda vacillated between deep sorrow and intense anger throughout the conversation. Now she was furious. "What cowards! Who runs away and leaves helpless old people behind to face a monster like Katrina? I just pray Grandma wasn't conscious for the end."

"I am so sorry," Martha reiterated. "All of us here will keep you and your family in our prayers. And please let us know if there is anything we can do. You know everybody here loves you." Martha could hear Linda sniffle on the other end of the line, and they spoke for a few minutes about the sheer devastation that Linda witnessed all around her. From what could be ascertained, the neighborhood where Linda's family had lived for three generations was, for all intents and purposes, obliterated.

"I have to get back to Mom now," Linda said. Dad is with her, but he's focused on getting us back home as soon as possible. He's not the best at caretaking, anyway.

"Okay. Well, please call again when you can, Linda," replied Martha. "I'll let the staff know what's happened. I'm certain David will try to call you." They hung up, and Martha left her office to share the sad news with Julia and the rest of the staff.

After news of Linda's loss had sunk in, a pall was cast over the entire office. The extra work and the wrecked lives that the storm had left in its wake were taking a toll on morale. And in practical terms, albeit nothing that was voiced, Linda's absence was proving to be a major hardship on the agency. David had recently begun pursuing a master's degree in social work, an effort that Martha supported. She had promised David some flexibility in his schedule when he first registered for classes. Now, she wasn't sure she could spare him at all. And with the influx of new clients due to Katrina, they were busier than ever.

Late in the afternoon Martha was sitting in the break room with David and Ruth, when she broached the subject of the impact of Linda's absence. She had just put in a call to Melissa, who had graduated with a bachelor's degree in social work in May and was working for the United Way. Melissa had agreed to work with them in the evenings when Ruth was teaching her class, but she couldn't spare any more time than that, as the United Way was also immersed in trying to meet the needs of Katrina evacuees.

"David, Melissa has agreed to work two nights a week," she told them. "You'll still be able to leave early and make it to class this semester. I don't know how long she can keep that up, but it does give me some time to see what happens with Linda. If she can't make it back in a month, we'll just have to hire a temp or perhaps even another full-time staff person." David was visibly relieved at the news of Melissa's help, and he thanked Martha for being willing to work with his schedule despite the circumstances.

Before leaving for the day, Martha asked Julia if she still had a copy of the ad they had run for David's position the previous year.

"You don't think Linda's coming back, do you?" questioned Julia.

"Well, I would be surprised if she did. Her family is going through so much right now. I think it's going to take a long time for things to get back to something even close to normal, and Linda clearly feels a need to be with her family. I wouldn't blame her at all if she stayed in Louisiana." She told Julia she would lock up, then turned off the lights and spent some time decompressing in the dark office.

The next day, it was business as usual at Helping Hands. Three people were waiting outside by the time they opened at eight. One person was there for help with her electric bill, while the other two were seeking rental assistance. At this point, Julia was skilled at screening people and could take care of vouchers for these items herself. It was a huge relief to David and Ruth, who were trying to focus on the clients who had more difficult issues or complicated situations, as well as the CNA trainees. Martha had developed a screening instrument that helped Julia ascertain fairly quickly, with just a few questions, if she needed to get a caseworker involved. She wasn't a social worker, and she didn't want to open a can of worms she couldn't handle, so she stuck to taking care of eligibility for services and providing vouchers to qualified clients.

As she was processing a request for a week's supply of groceries, Julia recognized Consuelo Hernandez as she came in the front door. Consuelo had completed both the CNA prep course and the community college program, and Julia recalled hearing Ruth say that she had obtained a full-time job in an assisted-living facility. When Consuelo asked to see Linda, Julia told her that Linda was on leave and asked if she would be comfortable talking with David.

"Well, I'd like to see Ruth if possible," Consuelo replied in her typically energetic manner. "She was the one who taught my class. But if she's not here, I guess that would be okay," she replied. "You all helped me so much when I was pregnant the last time. I wouldn't have my job without you guys."

"Pregnant *the last time?*" thought Julia. She wondered if that meant Consuelo was pregnant again. She surreptitiously caught a glance at Consuelo's left hand. There was no wedding ring, and while that didn't mean she wasn't married, Julia couldn't help but imagine that this young woman might now be jeopardizing her hard fought success with another pregnancy.

As Ruth was out of the office, Julia called David and found out that he was available. She then escorted Consuelo down the hall to his office. She returned to her desk, but was anxious to know the full story behind Consuelo's return to Helping Hands.

"Well," Consuelo began after David inquired how he could help, "a lot has happened since I finished the CNA program. My divorce was final about the time my son was born, and I haven't had as many problems with my ex-husband as I had before, but that's probably because he has a new woman. He does try to see Zeta, or Z, as we call him, sometimes."

Her face began to light up as she continued. "I have a new boyfriend, too! He's actually my best friend's brother. He's really nice, and he doesn't hit me. I've never even seen him lose his temper."

"What's his name?" David asked.

"Oh," she said with a smile, "Jeff. He works at the same place I do. We don't live together or anything, but we're expecting a baby in about five months." She was clearly excited about her pregnancy, but she did acknowledge that a new baby would make her plans to continue working increasingly difficult, since her job did not provide health insurance, and even if it did, she still wouldn't be able to afford childcare after the baby was born. She asked David if she would be eligible for any benefits from the welfare system.

David knew that Consuelo was asking about potential benefits from TANF and did his best to answer her questions.

"So, what specifically do you hope to get from the welfare program?" David inquired.

"I was hoping to maybe stay home with my kids, because I can barely afford the childcare I'm paying for right now." She told David that the six months of childcare support she received from Helping Hands after completing her CNA course had run out, and the cost for infant care was really high. David recalled his conversation about childcare costs with Martha and Melissa early on in the grant process, and knew Consuelo was not exaggerating.

Unfortunately, David knew enough about TANF to tell Consuelo her plan would not work.

"The state requires that you be seeking work or working in order to get TANF, Consuelo. Some states let people count short-term education hours toward the work requirement, but that wouldn't help you. And since you are already employed, there's a good chance that you make too much to receive any cash assistance." David felt that he was piling bad news on Consuelo, but he knew the welfare system was constructed to get people to work, not provide benefits to low-wage workers or mothers who wanted to stay home with their children. He tried to offer something positive, "You might be able to receive benefits for a few months after the baby is born. "

Consuelo interrupted. "So, you're telling me that if I want to stay home, I can't because I would have to work, and if I work then I would make too much to get assistance?"

"Well . . ." David hedged, trying to figure out a diplomatic way of describing the ambiguities in the system, "it depends on how much you make and how much you work. I mean, you might be eligible for food stamps or nutrition assistance from the Women, Infants, and Children program. There's also a Child Care Development Block Grant program that offers childcare subsidies, but the last I heard, there was a long waiting list for that. But let's say that you were to leave your job and sign up for TANF, you could be eligible for Medicaid. That would certainly help with your health care needs.

"But if the government wants me to work," Consuelo questioned, "why would I have to quit my job to get some benefits? I don't get it."

David practically slumped on his desk. "That makes two of us, Consuelo. But there's one more thing . . ." he said with hesitation.

"What's that?" asked Consuelo, incredulous to find out that there was more bad news.

"If you were to receive TANF before the baby is born, you wouldn't get any additional assistance for the new baby. Our state has a family cap."

"A family cap?" Consuelo asked, shaking her head. "What's that?"

David hated giving her such depressing news, but saw no way around the truth of the situation. He wanted to help her make the best decisions. "The state won't pay for any children born while the family is getting benefits."

Consuelo's confusion turned to indignation. "Like I'm having a baby for the money!" she said while shaking her head. "I guess I'll just have to keep working and try and find someone who would be willing to watch them. My parents aren't available except at night. They pick up Z now from daycare at five-thirty and watch him until eight. It's the daytime care I can't afford," she said, biting her lip. To David it looked like she was on the verge of tears.

"What about Z's dad, Consuelo?" David asked. "Does he pay child support?"

"Well," she responded quickly, "at first I had a tough time getting child support because he was unemployed. When he finally got a job, the Child Support Enforcement Office began taking some of his wages, and that really ticked him off," she said. "But now he's unemployed again, so I really can't count on getting money from him."

David nodded in understanding. Although the state Attorney General's office had made efforts to strengthen child support enforcement in the years after welfare reform had passed, many of his clients still received little or no financial support from the noncustodial parent.

"I'm going to check with Martha and see if there is anything else we can do or maybe some other programs I don't know about, okay?" said David.

Consuelo nodded her head but didn't look up.

"And it's not my place to give you advice or tell you what to do, Consuelo," David said. "But it sounds like you and Jeff are really excited about this baby. Maybe if you share this info with him, you can work together to come up with some ideas. I'll call you after I talk to Martha, okay?"

Consuelo gave David her telephone number and he walked her to the front door. There were no clients waiting for him in the lobby, so David headed straight to Martha's office. He hadn't known Consuelo when she had gone through the CNA class, but he did remember Linda saying something at a staff meeting about this young woman's resilient spirit.

David stood at Martha's door and gave a brief update on Consuelo's situation. "She's in a real bind now, with another baby on the way," he told her. "Even though we helped her with the CNA class and the six months of childcare, her wages just aren't high enough to pay for another infant's childcare while she works. And I know the system doesn't allow mothers to stay home and just take care of their kids."

"Well, historically, that's exactly what welfare was supposed to accomplish," Martha interjected, taking off her glasses and rubbing her eyes. "But over the years, more and more of an emphasis was placed on getting mothers into the workforce. That's really what welfare reform was all about."

"So welfare reform actually reversed the original intent of the program?" David asked with more than a hint of confusion.

"Well, there's arguments about it," replied Martha, "but that's what it seems like to me. And now mothers like Consuelo are caught in a bind—they make too much to qualify for most programs and not enough to truly make ends meet."

David took the conversation in a slightly different direction. "My policy prof said that states are taking matters into their own hands," he began. "She said that California just implemented a paid maternal leave program."

"A family law expert talked about it at one of the CCS meetings," Martha replied. "It provides six weeks of paid leave at about half of a typical salary. But considering that there are many countries in the world that provide a child allowance *and* more than a year of paid maternity leave, it's really just a start."

"Oh," said David. Martha could see she had taken a little wind out of his sails. Just then Julia walked up and stood next to David.

"Well," she asked David, "she's pregnant again, isn't she?"

Julia was clearly upset over what she had heard from Consuelo. "I just don't understand these young girls, having babies so early and not learning a thing from it. What was she thinking? She worked hard to get where she is, and now she's risking it all. I didn't see a ring on her hand, so I assume she's not married. Is this baby with the same man?"

"No . . . ," David replied with some hesitation. "She said good things about him, so maybe he'll be a responsible person and help her."

Martha knew that Julia's underlying issue was one that many social service providers face early in their careers. She remembered being frustrated and even sometimes hurt by clients for whom she had gone the extra mile, only to see them continue to make what seemed to be self-defeating choices that made no sense to her.

"Julia, I know how upsetting it is to hear about someone we helped do something we don't understand," Martha responded. "One of the lessons I learned early on is that I will only be involved with clients for brief parts of their lives, and my impact will most likely be limited. We don't control people's choices either, so all we can do is offer them our best professional help and hope that they use it well. When they don't do that, at least we know we did our best."

"Humph," Julia responded, putting her hands on her hips. It was clear she was not entirely convinced.

"Are you saying that you've had to lower your expectations, Martha," asked David. "That's what it sounds like to me."

"No, that's not what I'm saying, David. What I mean is that I hope for the best outcome and do my best to make that outcome possible. I just realize that our clients are human beings, influenced by us to a small extent compared to all the other things they have going on in their lives. Our clients don't always see things the way we might see them."

David told Martha that he thought that lesson just might save his sanity if he was to stay in the social work profession.

"I certainly hope so, David. I'd hate to see you give up and go back to selling drugs!" Martha joked, referring to David's previous career.

The joke broke the tension and they all roared with laughter at Martha's unexpected humor.

Questions for Discussion

1. Government statistics estimate that more than 1.5 million people evacuated their homes as a result of Hurricane Katrina. The sheer numbers of those forced to flee before or in the immediate aftermath of the storm has caused some to refer to it as the Hurricane Katrina or American Diaspora (see http://www.epodunk.com/top10/diaspora/index.html for a visual of communities across the country where evacuees eventually relocated). In what ways and to what extent was your community affected by Hurricane Katrina?

2. Aid to Dependent Children (ADC), the forerunner of TANF, was passed during the Great Depression as part of the Social Security Act of 1935. The

Personal Responsibility and Work Opportunity Reconciliation Act (PRW-ORA), which established TANF, was passed in 1996 during a period of extended economic growth. In what ways might the different economic and social circumstances of each period have influenced the differing objectives behind these important pieces of family legislation?

3. David and Consuelo discuss some of the features of the welfare system that were enacted as part of the reforms put in place by PRWORA. What do you know about the welfare system in your state? What are the time limits and work requirements? Is a family cap in place? What is the maximum amount of cash assistance available to a single mom with one or two children? What kinds of options would a single mom like Consuelo have in your state?

4. In this chapter, after Consuelo returns to Helping Hands to seek assistance and information, Julia is curious about Consuelo's present circumstances and asks David to share information he learned during his interview with Consuelo. Although David was hesitant to reveal details, the information he did share was a violation of confidentiality as Julia's position in the agency does not require her to know such details. Discuss the importance of and difficulties maintaining confidentiality in an agency setting.

5. David and Martha briefly discuss California's Paid Family Leave Law, an employee-funded benefit that pays workers up to fifty-five percent of their weekly benefits for up to six weeks to care for a new child or ill family member. While most Americans support the notion of family members being able to care for new or sick members, the argument typically centers on questions of eligibility, the duration and scope of family leave benefits, and how benefits should be funded. Discuss these issues in class. Can any sort of consensus be reached?

Innovative Assignments

1. A rich genre of film has developed in the aftermath of the Hurricane Katrina disaster. Some of the more prominent films include Spike Lee's *When the Levees Broke: A Requiem in Four Acts* (2006); *The Axe in the Attic* (2007); *Low and Behold* (2007); *Trouble the Water* (2008); the IMAX film *Hurricane on the Bayou* (2007); *Katrina's Children* (2008); and *Kamp Katrina* (2009). Although these films deal with the same subject, they each approach the disaster from different vantages. Write a critical review of two or three of these films. What are the similarities and differences among them? What do you think are the strongest points made in each film?

2. While New Orleans has received much attention regarding the damage it suffered in the aftermath of Hurricane Katrina, the brunt of Katrina's landfall on August 29, 2005, fell along the Gulf Coast of Mississippi. Even before the New Orleans levees broke, entire towns were wiped off of the

map in Mississippi, blown away by Katrina's fierce winds and washed away by her storm surge. Investigate and describe the damage that took place in other parts of the Gulf Coast and document the efforts that are being made to rebuild in those areas. In particular, investigate the impact that Hurricane Katrina had on important institutions like hospitals, schools, and social service agencies and examine the implications of service disruption among low-income populations in the effected areas.

Suggested Readings

Berman, E. M., & West, J. P. (1995). Public–private leadership and the role of nonprofit organizations in local government: The case of social services. *Review of Policy Research,* 14(1–2), 235–251.

Brinkley, D. (2007). *The great deluge: Hurricane Katrina, New Orleans, and the Mississippi gulf coast.* New York: Harper Perennial.

Dyson, M. E. (2006). *Come hell or high water: Hurricane Katrina and the color of disaster.* New York: Basic Civitas Books.

Heymann, J. (2002). *Can working families ever win?* Boston: Beacon Press.

Horne, J. (2008). *Breach of faith: Hurricane Katrina and the near death of a great American city.* New York: Random House.

John, K., & Montjoy, R. S. (2006). Incrementalism before the storm: Network performance for the evacuation of New Orleans. *Public Administration Review,* 66(1), 122–130.

Sothern, B. (2007). *Down in New Orleans: Reflections from a drowned city.* Berkeley, CA: University of California Press.

South End Press Collective. (2007). *What lies beneath: Katrina, race, and the state of the nation.* Cambridge, MA: South End Press.

Van Heerden, I. (2007). The failure of the New Orleans levee system following Hurricane Katrina and the pathway forward. *Public Administration Review,* 67(1), 24–35.

Winston, P., Golden, O., Finegold, K., Rueben, K., Turner, M. A., & Zuckerman, S. (2006). *Federalism after Hurricane Katrina: How can social programs respond to a major disaster?* Available at http://www.urban.org/url.cfm?ID=311344

CHAPTER 6

The End or a New Beginning?

JANUARY 2006

Martha sat at her desk, her hands wrapped around a steaming mug of coffee to warm herself from the chill of the morning. She could hardly believe that 2006 had arrived. In the fall, Martha had worked on a grant to obtain funding for enhanced casework services for Katrina evacuees, and in late October, after hearing from Linda that she was going to stay with her family in Louisiana, Martha began a search to fill the open caseworker position. Though Melissa had contributed some evening hours, they were not enough to make up for Linda's absence, and David's school schedule did not allow him to cover the extra hours. Helping Hands was falling short of service goals that had been set for the welfare-to-work program. To make matters worse, since the welfare-to-work contract ended in September, the insecurity about funding for the position further delayed the hiring process. It took Martha longer than she expected to find a qualified candidate who was willing to accept the risk that the job might not be re-funded. The new caseworker, Diana Rodriguez, was a mother of three who had spent the last few years staying home with her children until her youngest was school-aged. Prior to that, she had worked at a childcare facility after earning her associate of arts degree. There was much she had to learn, but she fit in well, and her ability to speak Spanish had already come in handy.

As Martha sipped her coffee, her thoughts wandered, in particular, to all that Helping Hands had done to support the Katrina evacuee population that had settled in River City. From the early days of supporting intake operations at the convention center shelter, the agency's involvement had shifted from short-term support to long-term planning to ensure that the evacuees had the services needed to adjust to their new lives in River City. Many Katrina evacuees from New Orleans had lost their homes, livelihoods, and family and community networks to the poststorm flooding. They needed everything from housing to employment, food and transportation—you name it, there was a need for it.

Martha reflected on the various struggles that River City faced in the months following Katrina. The first obstacle was finding housing for the evacuees living in the emergency shelter. While FEMA was able to pay for transitional housing for Katrina evacuees, there was a shortage of affordable rental properties available in River City. When the emergency shelter closed about one month after the storm, thousands of evacuees were sent to hotels as FEMA and local agencies tried to find more permanent housing for them. Martha and her staff had worked diligently with the other CCS agencies, meeting with landlords and property owners throughout the city to encourage them to be more flexible in their leasing agreements. Although it was now nearly five months since Katrina, quite a few evacuees were still living in hotels. "I can barely stand three nights in a hotel," Martha thought. "Imagine, months on end in a hotel room with multiple family members. Those walls would close in quickly on Allen, the twins, and me." But compassion for victims of Katrina was wearing thin in River City, and Martha winced every time she read an angry letter to the editor in the newspaper that blamed poor test scores, crime, unemployment, and a host of other problems on Katrina evacuees.

In order to develop a coordinated long-term recovery effort for Katrina survivors in River City, the CCS had held weekly meetings over the past four months. As CCS agencies had a long history of working together to minimize the duplication of social services across the city, they were committed to working collaboratively to try to meet the long-term recovery needs of the evacuees as efficiently as possible. In November, they had worked together to apply for a grant to provide case-management services to evacuees. Helping Hands and a couple of local nonprofits were identified immediately as the lead agencies for the grant due to their extensive history of case management with low-income populations. Martha had worked closely with the Executive Director of River City Advocacy (RCA), which specialized in advocating for the rights of individuals with disabilities, to write the grant. In early December they learned that their application had been accepted. Martha had spent the weeks before and after the holidays recruiting additional staff to run the program, though all the new workers except Melissa would work out of the RCA office.

Though the process had been tiring, Martha was ecstatic about the opportunity. It gave Helping Hands the chance to make a lasting difference in the lives of evacuees, and she was able to recruit Melissa away from the United Way to serve as the lead case manager for the grant. In fact, Melissa and Ruth had spent the past week in Baton Rouge, Louisiana, at a national training for the Katrina case-management program. Martha had scheduled a staff meeting for ten-thirty a.m. so that Melissa and Ruth could share the nuts and bolts of operating the program. Martha also wanted to make sure that it did not eclipse their existing priorities and continued implementation of the welfare-to-work grant. She knew the enthusiasm over the new program and the innumerable needs of the evacuees could potentially overshadow other clients if she did not maintain balance among the various services Helping Hands offered. Additionally, Martha was already thinking about reapplying for another two years of funding when the current welfare-to-work grant concluded at the end of September. She had to focus on changes she intended to make in services for the next round and begin preparing the application materials.

"Martha . . . Martha . . . oh, Martha?" Martha was slowly brought out of her thoughts by Julia as she stood at Martha's door. "Wow, guess that coffee isn't strong enough!" Julia teased as she walked into Martha's office.

"It's not a lack of caffeine," Martha said with a smile. "I just get lost in thought sometimes about everything that needs to get done around here."

Julia sighed. "After what we've been through the past few months, I'd rather be thinking on a warm beach somewhere!"

"Now you're talking," Martha concurred. Julia was raising two teenage boys by herself. If anyone needed a break, it was her.

Martha checked her watch and noticed that she only had about ten minutes before the beginning of the staff meeting. She gathered her things and walked with Julia toward the conference room, picking up Stan along the way. Martha thought it would be important for him to hear the information about the new program. When she arrived, Melissa, David, Ruth, and Diana were already seated around one end of the table, chatting up a storm, as usual.

". . . and you're not going to believe what else we tried while we were in Baton Rouge . . . fried alligator!" Melissa exclaimed, with pure enjoyment at the look of disgust that crossed David's face as she described the various delicacies she and Ruth had eaten on their trip.

"Fried alligator?" David said in horror. "Next thing you're going to tell me is that you ate one of those water rat things they have there. What are they called?"

"You're talking about nutria, *mijo*," Ruth responded instantly. "We're saving that for our next trip, right Melissa?" Ruth teased as she nudged her arm.

"Wow," Martha jumped in. "It sounds like you had quite a trip! Hopefully the case-management training was as exciting as the local cuisine." Martha smiled as she walked over to Ruth and Melissa, giving them each a big welcome back hug.

Martha and the rest of the staff were eager to hear about the training in Louisiana. They spent the next hour listening to Ruth and Melissa describe the principles of disaster case management as compared with traditional social services case management. They were glad to learn that all of the case-management forms, from intake to assessment to recovery planning, had already been developed by a national organization; but they were concerned about how much more work they might require and the impact the new system would have on service provision. They would also be documenting and tracking their case-management work through a Web-based case-management database. This was especially intriguing, as it would allow clients to move from one city to the next and have their case follow them without having to start from square one in each city. The database would also hopefully cut down on the duplication of services. They wrapped up the meeting by planning their schedule for the next two weeks, as Ruth would be starting a new CNA class in early February and the Katrina case-management program would open on February first. There was a lot to do in just two weeks, but at least it gave David and Melissa some time to show Diana the ins and outs of the welfare-to-work program.

The beginning of February arrived with an unusual warm front. Even though it was the first day of case-management services, word had already gotten out among the evacuee population. As Martha drove up the street toward the agency, she could see a line of people waiting for Helping Hands to open. As she pulled into the parking lot, she noticed mothers balancing babies on their hips, fathers holding young children's hands, and a number of elderly women sitting on the edge of the brick planting bed that lined the front of the building, fanning themselves in the surprisingly warm early morning February sun.

Martha quickly parked her car and hurried through the back door. "I can't believe we'll have to turn on the air conditioning in February!" she complained to herself. As she walked down the main hall and flipped the thermostat to cool, Ruth burst through the back door.

"¡Qué calor!" Ruth exclaimed, fanning herself dramatically with her hand. If this isn't global warming, then I don't know what is!"

Julia and Melissa arrived right after Ruth. "Can you believe the line out there?" Melissa inquired. "I guess we'll have to dive in head first today, eh Ruth?"

"Speaking of water," Martha said, "I don't want anyone getting dehydrated out there today. Let's get some bottled water out of the food pantry." She turned to Julia and took a $20 bill out of her purse. "Could you go get some bags of ice, Julia? The least we can do is offer some cold water while they are waiting."

A few minutes later Stan, David, and Diana arrived and were ready for business. Melissa walked through the lobby and opened the front door. A waft of hot, muggy air rushed into the room.

"Good morning everyone," Melissa warmly greeted the waiting clients. The line seemed to have grown in just the last ten minutes. "Please come in and get out of this crazy February heat. When the last person had squeezed into the lobby, Melissa asked, "How many of you are here for the Katrina evacuee program?" All but one or two raised their hands.

The number of hands made Melissa nervous. The day had just begun and there were already more clients in the line for the new program than she and Ruth could reasonably intake in one day. She excused herself for a moment and met with Ruth and Martha in the hall for a quick strategy session. Martha had already called the RCA and the receptionist there told them they were swamped too. At the meeting in Baton Rouge, Ruth and Melissa had been advised to schedule adequate time for intake assessments with Katrina evacuees. Martha knew from her experience at the River City Convention Center that assessments routinely took an hour or more. They agreed that they would have to set appointments for most of the group to come back later or on another day. Martha, David, and Diana then spent the rest of the morning in the lobby waiting area, handing out bottles of water, talking with the clients, and setting appointments for those who could not be seen that day. They assured those who had been rescheduled that there would be no negative effect on the services they would receive.

Once the scheduling was taken care of, Melissa called out the first name on the list. "Gwen Arnold?" A tall, African American woman of medium build stood up from the front line of chairs and gathered her purse. "That's me," she replied quickly. "I hope it's okay that I brought my daughter, Noelle. I don't have anywhere to let her stay while I'm here."

"Of course it's fine that she's here!" Melissa stated as she extended her hand in greeting. "I'm Melissa, a case manager here at Helping Hands. It's nice to meet you, Gwen." She smiled at Noelle, who immediately snuggled more closely to her mother. "How old are you?" Melissa playfully asked.

"She's two-and-a-half," Gwen replied as they started down the hall to Melissa's office.

Melissa shut the door and sat at her desk. "How about this weather?" she asked. "I don't know if it's February or July."

"I might as well be back in New Orleans!" Gwen replied as she wiped beads of sweat from her forehead with the back of her hand.

"Fortunately, this is not a common occurrence," Melissa explained. "Even those of us who have lived here all our lives are surprised by this." Melissa's dad always said that nothing was better at breaking the ice than talking about the weather, and in this case, it certainly seemed to be true.

Melissa then proceeded to explain her role as a case manager and the services that Helping Hands could offer Gwen as a Katrina evacuee. In order to assess her immediate and long-term needs, Melissa asked Gwen a series of questions about her experience with Hurricane Katrina and encouraged Gwen to share her story of surviving the storm and ultimately arriving in River City.

Gwen let out a deep sigh. "Well, I lived in New Orleans my whole life. I was raised in the Central City area, and all my extended family lived within five blocks. *All* of them."

"Really?" Melissa responded, while making a mental note of Gwen's close family situation.

"I am not kidding!" Gwen said with a smile. "I'm not saying that's necessarily a good thing, but that's just the way it is. Or the way it used to be, anyway," she said catching herself. She paused for a moment and then continued. "I have three kids, Samuel who's eleven, Rodney who's six, and my baby here, Noelle." Gwen smiled as she pulled a photo out of her purse to show

Melissa. "This is a photo we took a few weeks ago at the photo booth in the grocery store . . . I lost all the rest of our family photos in the storm."

A brief wave of despair shot across Gwen's face, but her composure returned a second later. Gwen shared that she and her family had lived in New Orleans for generations. She and her kids had shared the family home with her aunt Ruby. She and the children's father had separated shortly after Noelle's birth, and she needed the reduced housing and utility costs as well as the emotional support she received from her aunt. She used the public transportation system for work and to run any errands that required going outside their close-knit neighborhood. Facing Hurricane Katrina and losing a home that had been in their family for three generations was devastating for Gwen.

"I'm not gonna lie," Gwen leaned back in her chair and glanced up at the point where the wall met the ceiling. "It was worse than you could ever imagine. We knew the storm was coming, but we've lived in New Orleans our entire lives, so at first we didn't take it too seriously. Hardly anyone in my family has a car anyway, so we always try to make light of it, deep down knowing that we don't have many options to get out of town if it looks bad. We were pretty nervous once the city ordered mandatory evacuations, so we did pack a few things and went to the bus station, but no more buses were running. The people there told us that the bus drivers had skipped town to get out before the storm. So we just headed back to Aunt Ruby's and waited it out. I'm telling you, you have never heard anything like the winds that came through with Katrina. At first we were watching it out of the front window, but then we saw it tear off part of the roof from the house across the street, so we all ran into the hall closet and stayed there for hours. The wind was howling so loud, I couldn't even hear my own voice. I just kept hugging my kids close to me. Noelle slept the entire time, God bless her. Rodney kept crying, and Sam tried to act his best like a big man, but he was scared. Aunt Ruby and me, we kept praying Hail Marys; I mean, what else could we do? We must have said the rosary one hundred times that day."

Gwen paused, untwisted the necklace that Noelle had wrapped around her little hand, then looked up at Melissa and continued. She explained that the family had at first thought they had been spared any real damage. They awoke the next morning having survived the winds and rain, and the house was still standing. Then they realized something else was horribly wrong. Rising water was in the streets and began coming into the house. She assumed the levees had broken. Their only choice, due to the fast rising water and the inability for Aunt Ruby and Noelle to make it through the water to higher ground, was to carry some food and tools up to the attic, saw a hole in the roof, and wait for someone to rescue them as they waited on the top of their house.

"How long did you wait?" Melissa asked, her eyes wide as she internalized the traumatic events Gwen lived through. Melissa had heard similar stories during her recent training but was still horrified.

"It all starts to run together," Gwen said as she leaned back, shaking her head. "But I think it was about two days."

"Two days!" Melissa exclaimed, infuriated. "You waited for help on your roof with your children and your elderly aunt for two solid days?!" Melissa took a deep breath and leaned back in her chair, reminding herself to keep her emotions more in check. It was difficult, though, to look at little Noelle sitting there and imagine her stranded on a rooftop in the blazing sun for two days.

For the first time while telling her story, tears began to well up in Gwen's eyes. She wiped the tears, paused for a moment and continued. She told Melissa that Aunt Ruby got very weak as the hours passed. Gwen and the children also suffered in the heat and humidity, with no safe water to drink and very little food. She wasn't sure if they would survive another day and almost gave into despair. Finally, "miraculously," they were rescued by a man in his boat who took them to a city shelter. Although they went to the Superdome at first, it was clear they would not be able to stay there, due to overcrowded conditions, no working bathrooms or running water and a severe shortage of supplies. She said the smell was sickening, and she knew it would get worse before everyone was moved to better conditions. Gwen and her family were subsequently taken from the Superdome in buses to the airport, where she and the kids were separated from her aunt.

"Aunt Ruby was so sick that she was taken for medical treatment instead of leaving with us," Gwen stated. "They were even taking children and separating them from their parents."

Melissa experienced a range of emotions as she listened to Gwen's story. She asked what happened to the other members of her family, and Gwen said they were scattered around the country, from Houston to Nashville. Her aunt had been taken to a hospital in Houston, and then moved in with one of Gwen's cousins. Another cousin had returned to the city to see what could be salvaged, but Gwen knew many family members that were starting over in their new location. She herself felt lucky to be in River City.

Melissa listened intently as Gwen then told of her post-Katrina life in River City. She couldn't help but think of the stark similarities between Gwen and the clients she helped in the welfare-to-work program. Gwen described moving from hotel to hotel until she found an affordable apartment. Of course, they had no furniture, but at least they had vouchers to pay the rent. She had not yet found work, although she had applied at several different places. The biggest problem, even if she found employment, would be getting there each day. Her apartment was ten miles from downtown, and River City did not have the most reliable public transportation. Childcare, both during the day for Noelle and after school for the boys, would also have to be addressed. Melissa's previous experience in the welfare reform program prepared her well for Gwen's situation, and in spite of these obvious difficulties, Gwen continued to be hopeful that things would turn around soon.

Melissa and Gwen spent a few more minutes discussing Gwen's unmet needs, such as school clothing for the boys, diapers for Noelle, furniture for their apartment, and money for monthly bus passes for the whole family. With the clothing closet on site, Gwen could get items for the boys and Noelle while at Helping Hands. Melissa then went over the more difficult issues, such as employment and childcare as well as finding furniture for the apartment.

"We'll need to look into extending your FEMA benefits, and I know we'll have to work hard on that." Melissa had heard already from colleagues at the training that navigating the system was time-consuming and that clients would need help with that task. "The Salvation Army and the Red Cross would be a good place to start," Melissa continued. "They've donated furniture for Katrina evacuees at the Salvation Army, and the Red Cross might be able to help with buying a car."

Melissa was encouraged by Gwen's resilience and positive attitude. She wondered if the CNA program might work for her, but had not yet asked about her employment interests or the program itself. Gwen had said she worked in a department store in New Orleans, so the medical field could be a big shift for her. Melissa told her about the program and asked if she would be interested.

"I hadn't really thought of that before," Gwen responded. "I took care of some of my aunt's needs, since we lived together, but she didn't require too much. I guess it would mean working in a nursing home or someplace like that? Do you have anything I could read about the program?"

Melissa handed Gwen a brochure about both the CNA prep course and the RCCC certification program. "I do have to ask my director about eligibility for the program and make sure you would qualify. It's certainly possible, since you're a high school grad. We should explore it if you're interested," she said. "We don't have to decide anything today, and we can certainly look at other employment options too."

Gwen thanked Melissa for the information and said she would like to read the brochure and maybe talk to someone at the community college about the program. Melissa gave her Carol's contact information and suggested that she also inquire about other programs that RCCC might offer.

Melissa then set an appointment with Gwen for the following Monday so that they could follow-up on the employment opportunities and give Melissa time to meet with Martha about the CNA program. They stopped by the clothing closet, and Melissa played with Noelle while Gwen looked around. Gwen found a few outfits for her boys and took three packages of diapers for Noelle. She gave Melissa a big hug on her way out of the office, thanking her for listening to her trials and tribulations and expressing her gratitude for anything she could do to help her and her family.

After Melissa showed Gwen out to the lobby, she took a deep breath, a bit overwhelmed by her first Katrina case-management intake. She walked by David and Ruth's offices and noticed their doors were closed. With no time to waste, Melissa collected herself and called the next client on the sign-in sheet into her office.

Shortly after noon, the staff was gathering for lunch. Melissa, David, Ruth, and Martha were in the break room, each of them wanting to debrief on how the day was going. Martha told them she only had a few minutes to spare, as she had a lunch date with Carlene. Melissa recounted some of Gwen's story to her colleagues, especially the part about Gwen possibly qualifying for the CNA program.

"What do you guys think, would she qualify for the prep course?" Melissa inquired, hopeful to find a quick solution to Gwen's need for employment and childcare.

"I'm not sure, Melissa," Martha pondered the question. "It sounds like she qualifies from an income standpoint, but it's difficult unless she can verify her income. The Workforce Board rep is a real stickler for proper documentation. If she's not employed yet, does she have any means of showing what she's living on? You all know the bureaucratic nightmare evacuees have endured when trying to qualify for TANF without having necessary documentation." Melissa nodded knowingly, and Martha excused herself for her lunch date and told the group to keep working on solutions for Gwen.

"She has been bounced around so much since coming here that just getting a verifiable address wasn't even possible until a short while ago." Melissa sounded deflated. "I need to check into what exceptions can be made for evacuees around qualifying for services," Melissa said, still hoping the CNA program might work for Gwen.

"Good luck," said David. "The whole documentation thing is a nightmare. A lot of the government offices in New Orleans are still out of commission."

"It just seems crazy to require a person who lost everything to a disaster to provide documentation of any kind!" Melissa exclaimed in frustration. "This is a woman with three young children who has been shuffled from place to place for the past six months after seeing her home destroyed and barely making it out of New Orleans alive. Can't the government slack up on the rules until people get settled?"

Ruth reminded Melissa and David of a training they'd had right when the evacuees began arriving in River City.

"You guys remember them talking about how the feds are concerned about people showing up claiming to be evacuees when they really aren't?" Ruth shared. "I agree that it seems cruel to suggest people have documentation, but if they just give away rent, money, trailers, you name it, some bad apples are gonna take advantage of the system. And then folks will scream to cut the programs!"

"I wish they'd spend that kind of time investigating all the fraud that's taking place in Iraq and Afghanistan," David sharply replied. "They've given billions of dollars to contractors that can't be accounted for, and National

Guard troops that could have helped save lives in Louisiana were patrolling neighborhoods in Baghdad!"

David had become even more upset about the war after seeing the delayed and inefficient federal response to the disaster. But not everyone agreed with him. Unbeknownst to David, Stan had been standing in the break room doorway, listening.

"I don't agree with everything that's been done, by any means," said Stan. "But I do think Saddam had to go. He had been thumbing his nose at the U.N. for years, and everyone knows that you can't sit around and let a bully get stronger."

David composed himself quickly. "I would think that an accounting guy like you would be more upset than I am about the money that's been wasted," he replied.

"I spent four years in the Air Force right after Korea," Stan countered. "And I know the military does its best to be a good steward of taxpayer money. The money that goes unaccounted for is probably stolen by corrupt Iraqi officials or used to bribe the Iraqis or the Northern Alliance in Afghanistan to get them to do what they should be doing any way."

"Really?" said David, with a mixture of incredulity and escalating anger. Melissa gave Ruth an uneasy look.

"I think it's easy to criticize if you've never served and if you're not the one over there doing the dirty work," said Stan, leveling a solid gaze at David.

"Even if I wanted to serve, the military's "Don't Ask, Don't Tell" policy pretty much let's people like me know we're not wanted," responded David through pursed lips. "But they sure have no problem taking my tax money and giving it to Halliburton!"

"Okay guys," interjected Ruth in an attempt to keep the peace. "I think it's clear that you have different opinions. Let's just leave it at that." She gave them both a look. Stan nodded quietly and went to the freezer to take out a frozen dinner while David took his lunch and returned to his office. After a moment of strained silence, Ruth moved the conversation back to the task at hand. "Melissa, I'm going to call the Workforce Board rep and find out what we'll need to get evacuees certified to receive our welfare-to-work services. One of my clients told me she wants to stay in River City, too, so we need to get this figured out as soon as possible."

Across the city, Martha met Carlene at a deli close to the flower shop to catch up and discuss Martha's ideas for the welfare-to-work proposal.

"Do you remember the major parts of Dr. Barr's report that I shared at the board meeting?" Martha began.

"Yes, the lack of evening and weekend childcare was a big problem," Carlene replied. "I can't believe some enterprising person hasn't opened up an evening care center. There would be a huge market for it."

"The problem is that the people most likely to work in a childcare center also have families and want to be at home with their own kids in the evenings,"

Martha responded. "Even though there's a market for it, the labor isn't there to run it; and the folks who work the swing shifts can't afford to pay much for it."

"You're right, Martha," Carlene said. "Even if we wanted to offer it ourselves, we'd have the same problem finding staff. Didn't Dr. Barr also say that even though the CNA prep course is great and was helping people get through the community college program, that the wages people make still aren't high enough to move them out of poverty?"

"That's right. And even those who were officially above the poverty line had problems paying for rent and utilities."

"What was the term she used?" questioned Carlene.

"Continuing housing insecurity," replied Martha.

"That's right. Now I remember," said Carlene.

"But I think there's a way around the problem," said Martha. "RCC offers training in a variety of medical fields. Some of them, like dental hygiene, for example, offer better wages and more standard work hours. If we helped students get through those programs, we could kill two birds with one stone."

"But the training for those programs would have to be more extensive, right?" asked Carlene as she took a bite of her potato salad.

"You're right," replied Martha. "Some of the programs are one or two years long. And they all require a high school degree or GED to get in."

"If I remember correctly, isn't that called skimming when you only take people who have high potential to be successful even if you don't help?" Carlene asked.

"Close. Actually, it's called creaming or cherry-picking," Martha said, somewhat dejectedly. "I knew this was going to come up," she said shaking her head.

"Well if the shoe fits!" Carlene said sardonically.

"You know what?" Martha said, putting her palms in the air. "Guilty as charged. But every person we help would still be low income. And the more I think about this, why shouldn't we help those who are poised to make a go of it? So much of what we do is just emergency assistance. This is one way we could make a lasting, more permanent difference."

"Honestly, Martha," said Carlene with a reassuring smile. "I don't think the board would have a problem with it. But we would be talking about a much more intensive program, right?"

Martha smiled at her friend. "Yes, we would. We couldn't leave them hanging. We'd probably have to help them through the whole program, so we'd be serving fewer people and spending more money on those we served. There's no getting around it. But Carol tells me that graduates of these programs are starting at fifteen to eighteen dollars an hour, *plus* benefits. There's a lot of talk in welfare reform about promoting self-sufficiency. Well maybe it's time we do just that!"

"I think it would look good if you tied these proposed changes to what we learned from running our welfare-to-work program and as a positive response to the evaluation report," Carlene added. "You've really shown us what you can do Martha, both with this grant and with the new funding for the Katrina evacuees," she said. "I think the board will support you one hundred percent."

The two friends spent the remainder of lunch talking about kids and grandkids, and Carlene's hope that her son would be home from Iraq for good by June.

When Martha returned to the office, she entered the waiting room and saw Deena Perkins, one of their first CNA program clients, talking with Ruth. An attractive young woman stood beside them. Martha greeted them and asked how she was and how the job was going.

"I'm doing pretty good these days, since my daughter has come home," Deena replied. She introduced Martha to her daughter, Jackie, and said that they were at Helping Hands to enroll her in the CNA prep course. "We're hoping once Jackie finishes the class at RCCC, she can get a job where I work. Then we can take different shifts and share the childcare responsibilities."

"Sounds like a good plan!" Ruth interjected, obviously happy to see one of her former students making progress.

"I've also applied for a shift supervisor job at the nursing home, and I think I'm gonna get it," Deena continued with a great deal of enthusiasm. "The Perkins girls are just gonna take over!" she laughed, nudging her daughter.

Jackie spoke up. "It's a good thing we're planning to work different shifts, since having Mom as my boss at home is enough!"

Martha was happy to see that Deena's daughter was out of prison and that the family was coming together to heal old wounds and start a new journey. It was also gratifying to know that the welfare-to-work services that Deena had received at Helping Hands had made a real difference.

Over the next few months, Helping Hands served over 200 evacuee households through its Katrina case-management program. They assisted clients with everything from reinstating Medicaid, TANF, and food stamps benefits to helping them find permanent housing solutions and employment. They also connected them with training and schooling opportunities, and even helped some with their plans to relocate back to New Orleans.

Melissa continued to work with Gwen. She struggled with helping Gwen qualify for additional FEMA assistance because FEMA had determined that Gwen had not been the head of a household when she lived with her aunt. Melissa helped Gwen appeal this decision with FEMA. The process of working with Gwen and other evacuee families was a huge learning experience for Melissa. She gained a deeper appreciation for just how complex big bureaucratic systems could be and often commented to Martha how much she preferred to work in a small agency setting. Eventually FEMA did approve Gwen's request and she was able to get continued housing assistance and assistance to replace belongings from her damaged home.

One thing that Melissa did not expect and that particularly infuriated her was learning that Gwen's aunt Ruby had been charged for five months of water and sewage services for their damaged home in New Orleans, though the house had been ruined in the flood. Melissa worked with Aunt Ruby's case manager in Houston and contested the bill with the utility company. It was an exasperating process and served to remind Melissa that the list of issues affecting evacuees was literally endless.

On a positive note, Melissa learned that in response to the influx of Katrina evacuees, the Workforce Board had examined its policies about documentation and determined that Katrina evacuees able to verify their identity and whose post-Katrina income fit the eligibility requirement for the welfare-to-work program were eligible for programs funded under their auspices. This was wonderful information for a number of Melissa's clients. However, not surprisingly, Gwen decided shortly thereafter to move to Houston to be closer to her family. In addition to missing the close contact they had always had prior to Katrina, Gwen knew she needed her family's help if she were to try and further her education and work, even part time, while in school. She also decided that the CNA program was not the best fit for her, and after talking with Carol at RCCC, she chose to apply for a two-year fashion merchandising degree from a community college in Houston. Carol and Melissa helped her with the application process and with the financial aid assistance she would need to pursue her educational goals.

Martha and the staff continued to work on the welfare-to-work grant application, incorporating their experiences from the last two years of the welfare-to-work program and the more recent Katrina casework program. Martha was grateful to have a more experienced staff on whom she could rely to not only review the grant as she prepared it, but give her valuable feedback on key issues clients faced that might be resolved by the new grant. She knew that meeting basic needs such as food and clothing were critical to her agency's mission and could not be discontinued. She still intended to provide those services, while the consensus of the staff was that Martha's desire to assist individuals through additional degree and certificate programs at RCCC made good sense in light of Dr. Barr's evaluation findings. Though the "creaming" effect came up again when the changes were discussed with the entire board, Martha's resolve to move people toward true self-sufficiency ultimately prevailed, and the board approved the revised program application.

Martha was proud of the work she and her staff had put into the welfare-to-work program and the new application. Indeed, in many ways she thought it was stronger than their first application. The changes they planned in the new program were clearly linked to the evaluation data from Dr. Barr's report. Just as needs-assessment data was crucial in their first application, the second application made good use of the outcome data to justify the changes that

Helping Hands proposed for the next round of funding. A sample curriculum for a new prep course that Ruth planned to teach was included in an appendix to the application. Finally, Martha now had the luxury of budgeting for positions from different funding sources, which allowed her to use staff across programs when needed. Thus, personnel costs could be distributed among programs. She was able to show the Workforce Board reduced staff costs while increasing the services to a smaller group of clients with great potential. She only hoped that the reviewers from the Workforce Board would appreciate all they had done!

Over the last two years Helping Hands had increased the size of its budget, added additional staff members, and extended its reach in the community. Martha was well on her way to meeting goals she had established for Helping Hands when she had first become Executive Director years before. But there was still more to be done. Because the new program would increase the need for space, Martha had her eye on the recently emptied storefront next door. If they were re-funded, Martha envisioned creating additional classroom space and moving Ruth and other staff who worked specifically for that program next door. She knew that she could count on her staff, and that they would meet the challenges that most certainly were ahead.

In late June, just one month after submitting the application to the Workforce Board, Julia came into Martha's office with a large manila envelope in her hand. David, Melissa, and Ruth were right behind her.

"I think I know what this is," said Martha with a smile.

"I wanted to tear it open but Julia wouldn't let me!" joked David.

Martha took the package from Julia and pulled out her brand new letter opener. It was part of new desk set her kids had given her on her birthday.

"I can't think of a better way to break this in!" she replied with a laugh. "Here goes nothing!" Martha said as she opened the envelope and looked inside.

Questions for Discussion

1. In River City, the Council of Community Services worked collectively to prevent extensive overlap or duplication of services by member agencies. What are the pros and cons of minimizing duplication? Would you support such efforts in your town or city? Why or why not?

2. One comment frequently heard after Katrina was that residents of New Orleans should have evacuated before the storm. Discuss various reasons why some residents, especially poor residents with few resources, did not evacuate. Do you think the city, state, and/or federal government should have facilitated and organized the evacuation prior to the storm? Why or why not?

3. Dr. Barr's evaluation of Helping Hands demonstrated that graduates of the CNA program were employed but still struggling financially. Hence, Martha

wanted to modify the program to help support fewer clients advance in potentially more lucrative careers. What do you think of this decision? Is it the best use of resources? Under what conditions do you think "creaming" can be justified?

4. We hear again from Deena and meet her recently paroled daughter, Jackie, in this chapter. It is clear from the conversation with Martha and Ruth that to achieve a semblance of economic security, it is necessary for them to live together and share expenses and childcare duties. Similarly, Gwen chooses to leave River City and move to Houston to be near family. The support and childcare they can provide while she attends college is crucial. Both situations demonstrate the role that family plays in the United States. However, for various reasons, many households often cannot depend on assistance from family members. When family members are not part of the equation, what role should government policy play in supporting working families? If you think government should provide financial or material support, should it only be given to those who can demonstrate need, or should it be offered in a more universal manner, as it is in many other industrialized countries?

Innovative Assignments

1. Many survivors of disaster need help and support in adjusting to the "new normal" of life after the disaster. This is one of the major roles that case management plays postdisaster. Case managers help survivors to structure this process by working with them to develop recovery plans. Recovery plans identify the various unmet needs that a survivor has that are related to the disaster (i.e., housing, furniture, employment, rebuild assistance, etc.), the desired objective for each need, and action steps needed to reach each objective. The recovery plan also identifies the party responsible for completing the action steps and the timeframe during which it should be accomplished. Finally, the case manager follows up with the client to identify the outcomes of each objective. Develop a detailed recovery plan for Gwen Arnold, the client featured in this chapter.

2. Nonprofit organizations like Helping Hands play a huge role in disaster recovery efforts all across the country. These voluntary organizations often lead efforts in providing food, shelter, case management, and basic support to survivors. Review the following Web sites and catalog the number of ways in which these voluntary organizations work in disaster. On the basis of information that can be obtained from these sites, analyze the strengths and potential weaknesses each of these organizations possess in addressing the diverse needs of victims of natural disaster.
   a. American Red Cross: www.redcross.org

b. The United Methodist Committee on Relief (UMCOR): www
.umcor.org
c. Lutheran Disaster Response (LDR): www.ldr.org
d. National Voluntary Organizations Active in Disaster (NVOAD):
www.nvoad.org

3. One of the greatest challenges for host communities (communities that
hosted evacuees) in the wake of Katrina was finding sufficient safe and
affordable housing in which to settle the evacuees. Research the housing
situation in your city, identifying the various public housing programs available, the accessibility of affordable housing, and the challenges that low-
income populations have in locating such housing. Write a five to ten page
paper on the status of affordable housing in your city and how your city
would fare if it were faced with having to house hundreds, if not thousands,
of evacuees in a short period of time.

Suggested Readings

Auer, J. C., & Lampkin, L. L. (2006). *Open and operating? An assessment of Louisiana
nonprofit health and human services after hurricanes Katrina and Rita.* Washington,
DC: Urban Institute/Louisiana Association of Nonprofit Organizations.

Brown, T. L., Potoski, M., & Van Slyke, D. M. (2006). Managing public service contracts: Aligning values, institutions, and markets. *Public Administration Review,*
66(3), 323–331.

Gazley, B., & Brudney, J. L. (2007). The purpose (and perils) of government–nonprofit
partnership. *Nonprofit and Voluntary Sector Quarterly,* 36(3), 389–415.

Hartman, C., & Squires, G. D. (2006). *There is no such thing as a natural disaster:
Race, class, and hurricane Katrina.* New York: Routledge.

Morris, J. C. (2006). Whither FEMA? Hurricane Katrina and FEMA's response to the
gulf coast. *Public Works Management and Policy,* 10(4), 328–343.

Pipa, T. (2006). *Weathering the storm: The role of local nonprofits in the hurricane
Katrina relief effort.* Washington, DC: Aspen Institute.

Simo, G., & Bies, A. L. (2007). The role of nonprofits in disaster response: An expanded
model of cross-sector collaboration. *Public Administration Review,* 67(1), 125–142.

Smith, S. R. (2006). Rebuilding social welfare services after Katrina: Challenges and
opportunities. In E. T. Boris & C. E. Steurerle (Eds.), *After Katrina: Public expectation and charities' response* (pp. 5–10). Washington, DC: Urban Institute.

Stivers, C. (2007). So poor and so black: Hurricane Katrina, public administration, and
the issue of race. *Public Administration Review,* 67(1), 48–56.

Afterword

We wrote this book because we were inspired: inspired by the way communities, agencies, faith-based organizations, and caring individuals came together in the wake of welfare reform to create and implement entirely new programs to assist low-income families to help make ends meet; inspired by families struggling to overcome a plethora of burdens in the form of unemployment, lack of job or language skills, limited education, and domestic violence or substance abuse, to create better lives for themselves and their children; inspired by Katrina evacuees, authors, and filmmakers who will not let us forget the horrors visited upon the Gulf Coast by nature and government ineptitude and indifference, and by those who are helping survivors to rebuild their lives and reenergize communities devastated by the storm. And yes, inspired by students, advocates, and legislators who recognize that effective government policies are essential for a just society to advance the common good.

Students in the "helping professions" often approach the subject of social policy with anxiety or disinterest. Those whose main desire is to help individuals, groups, or families in a direct practice or clinical setting may underestimate the importance of public policy, policy analysis, and administration and community practice skills on their effectiveness as social service providers. On the other hand, students who are primarily interested in public policy run the risk of overlooking the myriad ways in which policies are implemented at the organizational and community levels and the importance of the human relationships that lie at the core of "street-level" service delivery. Thus, in the wake of welfare reform, it is critical to understand the diverse ways in which public policy links low-income clients to an assortment of organizational actors that have taken a larger role in delivering services to needy populations. It is also important to understand how direct-practice skills contribute to the effective implementation of public policy, be it at the organizational, community, state, or federal levels.

This book is based on a five-year evaluation of over forty welfare-to-work programs in Texas. The programs were first implemented during George W.

Bush's tenure as governor and continued through the years of his first presidential administration. As governor, George W. Bush emphasized the participation of faith-based organizations (FBOs) and, as illustrated in chapter 4, actually invited faith-based representatives of funded programs from around the state to a press conference announcing the start of "Welfare Innovation Programs." It is not a stretch to say that these programs provided a model that President Bush emphasized early in his first presidential administration through the establishment of the Office of Faith-Based and Community Initiatives. The most common services provided by innovation projects were financial assistance, usually in the form of housing or utility vouchers; educational programs such as basic literacy, ESL, and job-specific training; and transportation in the form of bus passes, gas vouchers, and vehicle repair. Most projects also provided substantial (and unfunded) in-kind resources, referrals to other community services, and limited case management.

Eligible program participants were required to be U.S. citizens or legal permanent residents; have one or more of their legal dependents (eighteen years old or younger) residing with them; and have a household income at or below 200 percent of the federal poverty level. Just as Martha and her team experienced, all but a few of the projects we evaluated were implemented in a short period of time and, perhaps as a result, the majority of projects required only marginal adjustments to the typical service orientation of the organization. Nevertheless, survey responses from program participants indicated a high level of congruence between the services that welfare innovation projects offered and the primary hardships clients faced. Overall, the local innovation projects expanded the capacity of their parent organizations to serve low-income populations by helping them to serve more individuals and families and, like Helping Hands and Rev. Anderson's childcare center, helped foster partnerships between organizations with similar missions. Though most projects offered limited assistance to meet a variety of emergency needs, the most successful projects identified full-time employment niches in the local workforce and provided sufficient training, resources, and support to enable program participants to compete for these positions and thus improve their economic well-being. Helping Hands' original CNA assistance program and support of additional degree programs in their new grant proposal are examples of this type of strategic planning and effective implementation in action.

Though the book focuses on the participation of a community and faith-based organization to deliver services in the wake of welfare reform and Hurricane Katrina, readers should not construe this as an attempt to advocate for a "takeover" of social services through privatization or the outsourcing of social services to community agencies or FBOs. There is a clear and pressing need for government at the local, state, and national levels to play a significant role in the financing and delivery of services to needy populations. But we also recognize that the variety of family and local economic situations, severity of need, and the sheer numbers of individuals seeking services would strain even the most efficient bureaucracy's ability to holistically meet client needs. Thus, it is clear that partnerships between government entities and private groups will continue to play a vital role in the nation's fragmented social welfare system. Our intention in this book is to shed light on the realities of these partnerships and provide evidence of the successes, failures, and limits of these approaches. We have seen the best and worst of these endeavors and have attempted to capture a reasonable expression of what takes place on a day-to-day basis through our story of River City Helping Hands and its partners.

The book is also based on three years of experience operating disaster recovery services in the Gulf Coast region in the wake of Hurricane Katrina. The story shared by Gwen in chapter 6 represents the struggles, confusion, emotions, successes, and failures of the Katrina recovery process for tens of thousands of Gulf Coast residents. Helping Hands' involvement in the Katrina recovery effort also represents the collective efforts put forth in communities throughout the nation to meet the emergency needs of Katrina survivors, and the contributions of many nonprofit organizations that have worked tirelessly to support the long-term recovery of survivors through the provision of case management, direct assistance, and rebuilding programs. Ultimately, the inclusion of the Katrina storyline as part of this book demonstrates the importance of coordinated collaborative work between all sectors of a community in the wake of disaster; and that community-based organizations, each with a unique history of reaching out to those in need, play an essential role in long-term disaster recovery work.

Finally, a note on the unique narrative style of the book. In our capacity as evaluation researchers and in our efforts to provide disaster relief, our lives were filled with stories. Welfare innovation projects were often administered and staffed by colorful characters whose roots ran deep in their communities. The cast of characters we interviewed included social service professionals, former oil executives who entered social service work as a chance to "give back," and ministers who viewed the welfare innovation projects as a way to provide assistance, not to "clients" in the strict sense of that term, but to parishioners, friends, and neighbors. In one of our evaluation visits, we observed drug deals taking place (ironically, while we were interviewing caseworkers in a substance abuse counseling agency); in another, a program volunteer thought it was important to show us where John Wesley Hardin, the notorious western outlaw, watered his cattle. We were also exposed to a tremendous diversity of settings: massive community agencies with multimillion-dollar operating budgets serving inner-city Houston; *colonias* along the Texas-Mexico border serving households with no running water or electricity; and rural towns of 400 with one paved road, staffed entirely by church volunteers.

Thus, to capture the drama and flavor of all that we experienced, we created a fictional composite of a welfare-to-work program based on the remarkable variety of real-life situations and characters we met and programs we evaluated. The characters in this book are a blend of the social workers, clients, social service professionals and faith-based community leaders we encountered over the years. We wanted our characters to face difficult decisions and challenging clients, to share inspirational and heartbreaking stories, and confront the bureaucratic red tape that inevitably challenges local programs funded with taxpayer dollars. In short, we wanted to inspire readers, especially students, in the same ways we were inspired. We envisioned students reading the chapters and animatedly debating an issue or asking one another how they would respond under similar circumstances. We deliberately included characters in our story who were much like our undergraduate and graduate students. In our story, Helping Hands staff frequently engage in policy level discussions with Martha, develop creative responses to client problems when the system put up roadblocks, and help to plan communitywide efforts to cope with a natural disaster. Through their eyes and those of the more experienced social service workers in our story, students see how they may be involved in policy and macropractice upon graduation, and we hope they will be inspired to make a difference in their communities and work settings.

In the end, we hope you enjoyed reading this book as much as we enjoyed writing it!

About the Authors

Miguel Ferguson, PhD, is associate professor in the School of Social Work at the University of Texas at Austin.

Heather Neuroth-Gatlin, MPA, is vice president for Lutheran Social Services Disaster Response (LSSDR) and has spent over fourteen years in nonprofit and public sector management. She has been involved in disaster recovery since 2006 and currently directs a FEMA-funded disaster case-management project for Hurricane Ike survivors in Texas. She resides in Austin, Texas, with her husband, Travis.

Stacey Borasky, MSW, EdD, is chair of the social work and sociology departments at St. Edward's University in Austin, Texas. She was the former principle investigator of a statewide child welfare training and evaluation grant with the state of Tennessee and has twenty years of experience in the child welfare arena as a social work practitioner, academic, and administrator.